M000317695

THE PLAYBOY
AND THE RAT

THE STORY OF JAMES HUNT
AND NIKI LAUDA

THE PLAYBOY
AND THE RAT

THE STORY OF JAMES HUNT
AND NIKI LAUDA

ROY CALLEY

This edition published in Great Britain in 2013 by DB Publishing, an imprint of JMD Media.

Copyright © Roy Calley 2013

All Rights Reserved. No part of this publication may be reproduced, stored in a retrieval system, or transmitted in any form, or by any means, electronic, mechanical, photocopying, recording or otherwise without the prior permission in writing of the copyright holders, nor be otherwise circulated in any form or binding or cover other than in which it is published and without a similar condition being imposed on the subsequent publisher.

ISBN 9781780910536

Printed and bound by Copytech (UK) Limited, Peterborough.

Contents

FOREWORD

When James Hunt stood on the third place podium step at the Mount Fuji circuit in Japan on a darkening Sunday in October 1976, there was nothing that would convince him that he had just realised his greatest ambition to become the Formula One World Champion. After a season of dramatic twists and turns, politics and retribution and too many hopes dashed in an unforgiving sporting arena, the thought that it would just as easily be cruelly snatched away from him the moment he allowed himself to believe was uppermost in his mind. It was only once he had returned to the press room and studied the lap charts and noticed that most people had departed the now ever-gloomy race circuit that he finally acknowledged that his hard fought and almost fortuitous third place had given him enough points to take the World Crown in a title race that he had never at any stage led during the season.

At the same time, the man he had fought so valiantly, Niki Lauda, was on his way to Tokyo airport. He had been ahead of the World Championship throughout the season and had gone into the final race still favourite to retain the Crown he won in 1975, but at the soaking Fuji circuit, Lauda had self-preservation at the forefront of his mind. He had literally come back from the dead after a fearsome and terrifying crash at the notorious Nurburgring circuit in Germany in August, and after being given the Last Rites in hospital, had somehow returned to the cockpit just six weeks later in Italy to continue the seemingly relentless and almost irrelevant fight. The rain in Japan stopped it and him and he walked away for that season, unable to defend the onslaught that was Hunt, the only time he had given up.

For James Hunt it was the highlight of a breakneck speed career that had catapulted him to motor racing stardom at a seemingly indecent haste and one which he had embraced fully both on and off the track. It had given him life's rich pleasures and he had indulged without abandon, but soon it faded away as uncompetitive cars and eventually a fear of death brought his career to a halt within three years. His life then spiralled out of control with a combination of alcohol, drugs and too many women bringing about financial disaster, leading to his far too early death at the age of just 45. Forty five years that had been lived to the utmost and had seen more packed into them than most.

For Niki Lauda 1976 was just a footnote in a long and successful career. He had already won the title in 1975 and then went on to win it again in 1977 before retiring, only to come back and win it once more seven years later. Once he walked away from the sport for good twelve months on, he never looked back apart from a brief time as a F1 team manager – and went on to create a new career with his airline businesses, fighting the huge Austrian Airlines with the same vigour and relentlessness that encapsulated his racing life. Now a millionaire and an elder statesman of the sport, he could not be any more different from Hunt, yet the two had forged a bond and a trust down the years. This is their separate stories that overlapped and entwined in unison, but had stunningly different endings.

CHAPTER ONE

Childhood and growing up

It is easy as the passage of time collates to add a certain lustre to a person's image, and certainly many have done so with James Hunt in particular, but when his Mother, Sue, said that she knew from the moment he was born that James Simon Wallis Hunt would be something of a rebel, then it was clear that his life would not be ordinary. Born on the 29th August 1947 and eventually one of six brothers and sisters born years apart, he was undoubtedly the one who would cause the most concern and create the biggest waves in his life. He was described in his early years by his mother as 'unmanageable' and was the only one out of Sally, Peter, Timothy, David and Georgina who would regularly escape from his cot and spend the whole evening screaming for no apparent reason. He was not a happy child and he himself described his young persona as a 'very difficult boy'. His quest to always get what he wanted, be it a desired toy or a trip somewhere would take his behaviour to extremes, eventually grinding down his parents 'like a steady drip, drip, drip' as it was described.

One can only feel the utmost sympathy for his Mother and Father, Sue and Wallis. Two self respecting and devoted parents who in the post war years had raised a family in a Victorian image of obedience, self-discipline and respect. That Victorian attitude precluded affection, but that in no way suggests that there was no love from parent to child, it was just not a household that would show it openly. This was something that in later years James would point to as a way of explaining and excusing his overindulgence and lack of attention with and for the opposite sex.

Sue was a loving mother who after bringing up her six children then immersed herself into charity work in Cheam and later Sutton after they had moved. Wallis, who she had met on a blind date, had attended Sandhurst, and while she was on duty with the Wrens, he had war duty with the 11th Hussars regiment. Following the end of the Second World War, after travelling the globe with an international trading company, he became a senior partner in a successful London stock-broking firm, but an internal fraud of which he was totally unaware liquidated the firm and so heavy losses followed. He recovered from the setback and found more success with an accountancy firm. It is fair to say that the resoluteness of Wallis certainly rubbed off on his youngest son and made him the man he became.

That man took some time to arrive though. As a child James was frequently in trouble and on one well-documented occasion he received a thrashing at the age of four for hitting brother Pete over the head with a shovel which was a portent of things to come. Schooldays seldom helped as he would spend most of the journey there screaming as the dark and foreboding building neared. He hated the confinement and the rules and the discipline and just about everything that was schooling. It became worse inevitably when he was sent to boarding school in Hastings at the age of seven, and one can only imagine the torment his mind experienced as he watched his parents disappear for the next few months. How he survived unscathed is unexplained, but he did excel at sports and knitting. The sports are easily understandable as he was incredibly athletic, majoring in cricket, tennis and running, yet the knitting was one of his more curious skills. To pass the time away, he decided to knit his brother Tim a pair of shorts, not to a perfect degree as he had managed to create two right legs, but they were rightly and proudly presented to Tim who kept them for some time. There is no evidence to suggest they were ever worn!

His interest in cars came at about the same time as his interest in women. The car, or rather a tractor, captivated James on a family holiday at a farm in Pembrokshire. After mastering the art of changing gear, he progressed to an old battered Rover that he would race up and down a private road. The bug had caught hold of him early.

The women soon followed. In fact at the age of 12, one year after discovering cars, he fell for the teenage under-matron at boarding school. She certainly didn't discourage his attention and that was followed by an Australian au pair who had been brought into the Hunt household. His two abiding passions had taken hold early in his life.

At such an early age though, he wasn't it seemed in control of his destiny as numerous careers were mapped out for him and it was just a case of which one would attract. There was a suggestion he would follow his father into the army, but that was a fleeting moment and was quickly followed by a desire to enter the medical profession. It had more to do with the fact that a surgeon who removed his appendix drove a Rolls-Royce as opposed to any calling to help his fellow man, but he took and eventually passed the exams for a teaching hospital, and found himself at St Bartholomew's. For Hunt it was a tedious waste of time and he counted down the days until the holidays. Inevitably his 'interest' in all things medical ended once he had found his love of motor racing and 'St Bart's' were informed by letter one day that he would not in fact continue his studies as he had found a new profession to pursue. That profession was motor racing.

At around this time he met his first full time girlfriend, Taormina Rieck, a girl he met at the age of 15. For years they became inseparable and she would follow him as he pursued his other sporting interests such as tennis and squash, but like many others who followed, she saw a flaw in his personality that made commitment almost impossible and she finally left him when his constant unfaithfulness became an obsession and she could no longer stand by and watch it take place. This was the teenager and then the man who was James Hunt.

Niki Lauda could not be described as a rebel, but more of 'square peg in a round hole', which is the way the man spoke of himself in later years. He was born to rich parents as Andreas Nikolaus Lauda in Vienna on the 22nd February 1949. His mother, Elisabeth and father, Ernst-Peter were part of a family that had made its fortune in the paper industry and 'Niki' and his brother Florian were unsurprisingly expected to continue the family business. Niki though had already eschewed the luxuries and opulence that came with Viennese life in the post war years and seemed to have more in common with his grandfather Ernst who was a total anti-socialist and enjoyed a much more enjoyable lifestyle in St Moritz and also Lower Austria. It was Ernst who seemed to be modelling the young and impressionable Niki Lauda until one day Niki saw a glimpse on television of 'Old Lauda' receiving an award by the socialist government of the time. Outraged and for the first time sensing an illogical reasoning to what was taking place, he immediately sent his grandfather a letter reproaching him for such an action. His idolising of 'Old Lauda' ended at that moment and was cemented some months later when in front of the family, Ernst proceeded to humiliate Niki with the contents of the letter. From that moment, Niki Lauda was quite simply his own man and decided that whatever he wanted, he would get by himself. It wasn't always that way in the future though.

Schooling was actually an enjoyable affair for him as he refused to allow the process of learning to interfere with his life. He failed his third-year exams twice so that his parents enrolled him into a special school to do a university entrance course in a beleaguered attempt to get the boy interested in business. It was a failure as like Hunt, Lauda discovered cars at an early age. He had bought himself a 1949 Beetle for 1,500 schillings after realising that he enjoyed parking the guests' cars when they turned up at the Lauda mansion for dinner. He treated the Beetle with little less respect and destroyed it after launching from a ramp and flying for twenty-four yards before it fell to the ground with all four wheels splayed outwards.

No examination was sat, as his love affair with four wheels continued and in an act of almost desperation, his parents sent him off to become an apprentice mechanic. The die was cast and Lauda's love affair with cars was to match anything that could affect Hunt's life. The women for Lauda came a little later.

Sadly his brief dalliance with mechanical engineering ended prematurely after causing a complete engine rebuild following a botched oil change, something the other mechanics constantly teased him about. He decided that the only way to blossom his love of the motor car was to pass his driving test. He also promised his father he would return to college and pass his twice failed exams and was promised by his grandfather that if he succeeded at English then he would buy him a small car. He passed it but the car never came. Another moment of tension between the two.

As it turned out he almost immediately lost interest in 'tiresome academic qualifications' as he called them and decided that he had no idea as to how to gain them, that was until a girlfriend at his school graduated easily and another friend suggested they could 'doctor' the diploma so that it looked like his name at the bottom instead of hers. It was such an amateurish job that when Niki showed his parents the accused piece of paper, he kept well away so they couldn't study it too closely! It worked however and his parents delighted in the success of their firstborn son and showered him with financial gifts in the hope that he would now mature into the young businessman they had dreamt of. Their dreams were shattered with unseemly haste as it was clear to Niki that the money could only be used for one purpose, and that was to fund his new passion for all things motor racing. The bug had hit him at about the same age as Hunt and they had both defied family and peers to pursue an interest in a sport that was at its best peripheral and its worst, damningly dangerous. The only thing that Lauda didn't have was an insatiable appetite for the opposite sex.

For both the start of their love of motor racing came as an almost fleeting diversion. Hunt had attended a Silverstone meeting shortly after he had passed his driving test at 17 to watch the brother of his tennis partner Chris Ridge compete in a Mini he had prepared himself. It was a 'wow' moment for the young man and from that time he decided he would be a racing driver and then World Champion.

For Lauda there was no such 'Road to Damascus'. He just loved driving fast and although the great Jochen Rindt was making a name for himself not only in his homeland Austria and of course around the World (he became the first and so far only posthumous Formula One World Champion in 1970), Lauda had no affiliation to him or indeed the sport as a whole. He just wanted to drive cars fast. It was something they would both do in the following years, yet with varying degrees of success.

CHAPTER TWO

Cars, the early years

James Hunt would often say in the years that followed that getting his driving licence was when his life really began. The freedom of having a car that could allow him to break from the shackles was something that transformed his life, not that he took any care in nurturing this new found release.

He passed his test with consummate ease, according to him anyway, but once the examiner got out of the car, Hunt raced away 'like a lunatic' and then decided the only way to drive was flat out and he became 'a bit of a terror on the road'. His then girlfriend Taormina, or 'Ping' as she had become affectionately known recalled that era as 'madness, total madness'. Hunt drove recklessly everywhere and it would not be unusual for him and his friends, Chris Jones being one of the main accused to have a few drinks in the pub, and in those pre-breathalyser days, drive around in a souped-up Mini or MG at breakneck speed with James hanging on to their tails.

His control in the car was not something that could be taught, it had to come from experience and that experience saw him wipe out two of the family vehicles in quick succession. The first was a Mini van after rounding a bend at too fast a speed and subsequently rolling it for 50 yards, ending upside down in a bed of roses. That was almost a metaphor for his life!

James was shaken and his parents decided not to replace the van in a vain attempt to slow their son down and hopefully prolong his life. Within six months he did it again after borrowing the Fiat 500 they had acquired as a second family car. It only had a top speed of 50mph, but James used that to its full and proceeded to wrap it around a lamp post after a drunken dash through the streets with Chris Jones and having to take evasive action to avoid a stationary car in the middle of the road. Well that was the story he had recounted to his father when presenting himself in the early hours of the morning. Suffice to say Wallis was suitably unimpressed. It was then that the famous 'Hunt the Shunt' title was first used, presumably by a family member, but it was one that was to follow him around the racing circuits in years to come.

Despite all of this, Hunt never hurt himself in any of the accidents, either major or minor. In fact his first major injury was on a skiing trip in Switzerland with girlfriend 'Ping'. They had set off from the UK in a £10 Morris Oxford that got them as far as Verbier before as James put it: 'the old banger breathed its last'. Then the Swiss transportation safely got them to their destination for a fortnight of fun and frolics in the snow. Sadly for James he returned home with an arm in a sling and in some pain. It didn't come from any unfortunate skiing accident, but rather from falling from a balcony and a break to his shoulder, which in later years would explain the slight stoop to his gait as he walked. It meant his frenetic driving had to be curtailed for a while and it was at this time that his 40 cigarettes a day habit was introduced to his life. Amazingly it never seemed to affect his fitness during his motor racing years, something which seems almost inconceivable today.

He had been introduced to the sport of motor racing after the trip to Silverstone, and like most things in his life he embraced it with an all-consuming passion. He had decided that he not only wanted to be a racing driver, but was going to become Formula One World Champion, without any knowledge of how this was to come about. After writing to St Bartholomew's tendering his resignation, he approached his father with a rather radical, if not quite presumptuous, idea. He reasoned that it would cost his parents around £5,000 to put him through medical school, so to save them money, he would take half of that so that he could fund his new passion and start racing. It is fair to say that father Wallis didn't quite flow in unison with James on this one and the money was unsurprisingly not forthcoming. Instead he paid for James to attend a racing driving course at the Brands Hatch circuit in Kent, mainly in the hope that it would get the racing bug out of his system. Sadly for him it failed, and for James it was a complete waste of time as he hardly shone, believing that the money could have been put to better use buying his own machinery. That was the single-mindedness that described James Hunt throughout his life. If he thought he knew better, then he would simply just go ahead and do it.

Another example of that 'selfish' nature that was part of his complex personality was his refusal to conform to what most regard as 'normal' standard of dress. He had never been smart and would often walk around in a v-neck sweater and ordinary trousers when most of the 60s hippy culture (in London especially) would gladly parade a tabard of riotous colours in their everyday demeanour. As the years went by and James Hunt became more and more his own man, his dress sense would amuse and appal in equal measure. There will be more of this later, but turning up at very expensive awards ceremonies in a tatty T-shirt and faded jeans with no shoes was the norm as opposed to the exception.

Niki Lauda used his graduation prize to buy a car. It was inevitable as by now it was the only passion he had. He bought another VW Beetle and thrashed that around the roads in an attempt to elicit as much speed as he could from the ageing vehicle. Of course he was likely to crash and his first encounter with the sudden impact that a travelling vehicle can have at high risk speed came, but not in his car. He'd borrowed his school friend's father's Mini Cooper S and promptly skidded on an ice patch and rattled the car against a bridge parapet. It was damaged badly and Lauda had no choice but to offer to buy the car as the idea of trying to explain the accident and the reasons as to why he was in the car in the first place were too dreadful to consider, so it was from that moment that the young Lauda found out about debt. He'd rushed around to his benevolent grandmother who loaned him the money and he then found himself with an old and unreliable Beetle, a badly damaged Mini Cooper and around 38,000 schillings of debt already. It was something which was to haunt his life for a few more years to come.

It was at this time that Lauda really decided that his future lay in the uncertain life that was motor racing, and to that end he visited the man he described as the 'Mini-King' Fritz Baumgartner. He was one of the great personalities of Austrian motorsport and had recently advertised his Mini Cooper S racing version for sale and of course that hooked Lauda instantly. As Niki said in his autobiography, 'I drove out to Baden where his car was garaged and looked it over. It was a dark blue version minus engine. Baumgartner saw me nosing around the car and came over to say hello. To me, he was some sort of god'.

Well Lauda did a deal with this 'god' after inviting him to his parent's palatial mansion and sold his Beetle, then traded his now-repaired Mini plus a heavy cash payment. Suddenly he had gone 'zero to racing car' as he put it, and despite the debts he was accumulating, he had found his 'calling' in life and did everything he could to follow his dream of being a racing driver. His parents, still misguidedly holding on to the belief that he would follow their footsteps into the paper industry and business, watched with amusement and indulgence as their younger son tinkered in the garage with a racing car. He had told them that he was only interested in the mechanical workings of the engine and had promised them faithfully that he had no intention whatsoever of racing the car ever as it was the last thing on his mind. His first race came just two days later on the 15th April 1968.

CHAPTER THREE

Let the racing begin

Lauda's debut race was actually a hill-climb at a place called Muhllacken in Upper Austria. He was accompanied by his mentor/sponsor Fritz Baumgartner, probably more for reasons of safeguarding his investment as opposed to any paternal feelings for the young debutant. Anyway, the new and naïve Lauda acquitted himself quite well with a second place finish overall after the two runs. It was certainly a hint that there was a modicum of talent and Lauda's belief that he could make a living out of the sport was enhanced by his performance. Sadly his father learnt (possibly through Baumgartner) that his son had just risked life and limb racing at crazy speeds and he expressly forbade him to do such a thing again. Baumgartner collected the money that was due to him and faded away from his life, presumably unwilling to get too involved in the family affairs of Niki Lauda.

Of course Niki did race again, just under two weeks later, at the next hill-climb at Dobratsch. He'd borrowed a friend's BMW with a trailer and a little money and with his girlfriend Ursula Pischinger he drove through the night to attend. It was worth it as he won his class and the Lauda-machine was well and truly rolling. Again though his father failed to appreciate the talents of his son and the row that followed led to years of estrangement between the two. Lauda moved out of the family home and immediately into the arms of Mariella Reininghaus in Salzburg. How this came about is something which Lauda has never made public (and why should he?), but it seems he had met her whilst on a skiing trip in Gastein when he had quite literally fallen for her! In fact he had fallen over quite spectacularly at her feet and they had bonded from that moment and not long after shared the tiny apartment in Salzburg.

The break up with the family gave Lauda the space to now pursue his dream of being a racing driver. It became all-consuming and a passion that overwhelmed everything else, yet why that should be was a mystery to the man himself. He had no racing idols, even Rindt hadn't really affected him in either life or death, and a week before his debut race/hill-climb, the great

Jim Clark had been killed in a Formula Two race at the Hockenheim circuit. Despite the public outpouring of emotion surrounding the event, Lauda had looked upon it dispassionately and gave no thought to the fact that he was entering possibly the most dangerous sport in the world at that time. It was just what he wanted to do.

Soon he had traded in his Mini Cooper for a faster and more purposeful looking Porsche 911 (also financed by his grandmother and a bank loan in fact he had no problem raising cash from the bank due to his family name) and spent the year racing around the country, with Mariella in tow. He was very successful, winning five out of nine hill-climbs and races and started to attract the attentions of various team owners who were looking for new and raw talent. He answered both those descriptions and as his prize money had helped to pay off some of his early debts, he took the next step necessary. He moved up to single-seater racing.

At the end of 1968 he tested a Formula Vee car for the Kaimann team and impressed enough to be offered a contract to race for them the following year, something which he did with surprising and impressive ease. He finished fourth in his first race at Hockenheim, but then suffered a dreadful accident in Vienna at the next race, ending upside down with an unconscious Lauda blissfully unaware of the danger around him. It didn't seem to faze him though as he said: 'I was completely crazy and hungry for victory. I tried to overtake where it just wasn't on'. It was that self analysis that kept Lauda as unemotional and unaffected as he climbed the ladder of motor sport success in the years that followed. Few were like him, and for that reason, few were as successful too.

That analytical mind was a trait that was unusual and almost unique in the 1960s racing driver's personality. Few had put as much thought into what they were doing, and most lived by the devil-may-care maxim that typified the racing driver image of that era. Lauda was different. He would reconnoitre the track beforehand and study its every gradient and camber, almost driving the race in his mind before the physical act of doing so, something which is a must in the current age, but at complete odds with the more carefree period he started in. It paid dividends as by the end of the decade he had recorded two wins in Formula Vee and although not spectacular, was solid and committed enough to be taken seriously by the people who mattered in the sport, the team managers and owners. As 1970 approached, he too was approached to move up to Formula 3, the final stepping stone to the dizzy heights of Formula One Grand Prix racing. He did it alone though, buying a car that put him in even more debt and travelled the country with his racing car on a trailer. F3 was an incredible place to be after just two seasons of racing, and he was determined that no matter how much money he owed, and it was a huge amount at that time, he would not worry about it and just let destiny play its part. From having little knowledge of this crazy sport in 1967, he was now just a trophy away from the pinnacle and he felt that 1970 would be a literally make-or-break year for him with racing and his increasingly fragile finances. Unfortunately, 1970 was a disastrous year in the life of Niki Lauda the racing driver.

James Hunt's attempts to become a racing driver almost sound comical today, but when he declared he would become World Champion, he was deadly serious. Of course he had absolutely no knowledge of the sport, never mind how to prepare any type of racing car, but that would not be a hindrance in any way. He decided that it would take him two years of odd-jobbing – delivery boy, ice-cream salesman, supermarket shelf-stacker – to earn enough money to buy his own car and get it ready for his racing debut. That car, like Niki Lauda's, was a crashed Mini, but unlike Lauda, its preparation left a lot to be desired. To continue funding his new obsession, he took on a job as a bus conductor and then a telephone salesman – all of it to pay for the pride and joy of his now total focus and interest. He cut down on his smoking, his drinking and his wild socialising just to feed the ambition that sat in the garage at home.

Eventually he put enough money by to pay for an engine to be installed, and then took the bald tyres and cut a tread in them himself before testing the car up and down the streets around his home. There were no windows in the car, so it must have been a breezing experience and as the regulations insisted on a passenger seat, he just screwed a deck-chair to the chassis with brackets from a Meccano set. He was ready for his race debut at the Snetterton circuit on a sunny summer's day in 1967.

Although James Hunt the racing driver was ready, there was no way the scrutineers were ready for him and they promptly saw the car and refused his entry. It was a devastating blow to the young Hunt, although his efforts were so unbelievably amateurish that it is inconceivable that he truly thought he would be allowed to race. No matter, as at the time Hunt took the rejection so badly that he promptly 'burst into tears'. He walked around the paddock in despair and declared that he was 'a broken man'.

His desperation was his parents' delight as they saw him come home in one piece, both of them totally convinced that James would kill himself in the car. Sadly for them, any misguided belief that he would now abandon this crazy notion of being a racing driver ended almost immediately. All the humiliation he had endured served to inspire him more and he finally acquired the funds to bring his racing Mini up to the regulations that were required. He finally made his debut at Brands Hatch on the 8th October 1967, retired the car in a plume of smoke and had two more rather unsatisfactory races in the car that year before persuading a fellow racer to buy his laughingly uncompetitive 'racer' for £325. The time as a telephone salesman had clearly not been a waste!

His 'wheeling and dealing' that followed saw him find enough money to move up to the single-seater Formula Ford category, a new level of racing that had been introduced the previous year to supply a cheap and price-capped form of racing. It was to be the making of him in the sport. Purchasing a Russell-Alexis Mk14 car for £345 plus £30 a month on hire purchase, he entered virtually every Formula Ford meeting in 1968. The money he paid had left him virtually penniless, meaning that often his 'bed' for the evening would be the unappealing floor of a press room at whatever circuit he was racing at, as a hotel was an extravagant luxury he simply could not consider, but on the track his ability started to shine. Mindful of accidents, mainly because he would not have the money to pay the repair bill, he found that he could easily be competitive and actually won his second race at Lydden Hill. With other good results throughout the year, including a lap record at Brands Hatch, it was clear that James Hunt had found his calling. Unfortunately he also had to find the money to fund his new profession and days of 'knocking on doors to get sponsorship' followed with little success.

One company did show interest though and that was Gowrings of Reading, a car dealer who ordered him a new FF car for the remainder of the season, with a view to running it full-time in 1969 with their name plastered all along. That partnership was brought forward though when Hunt destroyed his original car at Oulton Park in a huge accident involving a close friend, Tony Dron. They were fighting for third place when Dron hit trouble and as Hunt attempted to avoid the slowing car, he literally launched himself into the air, smashed through a Shell advertising hoarding, cartwheeled for yards before plummeting into the lake that formed the centrepiece of the circuit. Dron quite rightly thought that his friend was dead and went running after the car that had exploded all along the circuit until nothing was left and then saw parts of it submerged under the water. Fearing the worst, he was ready to dive in until James re-appeared from beneath the waves, bloodied and in a state of shock. No fiction film maker could prepare a better scene, but it was a testament to James' fortitude and sheer willingness that the first thing he did when laid down on the floor was to tell Tony Dron a dirty joke! James later said that the accident didn't worry him too much because he was 'young and stupid', but he seemed more distressed by the loss of his car which was sold for scrap metal and still had to be paid for. Motor racing was an expensive sport even in the 1960s.

The following year saw Hunt compete both in the UK and on the Continent in his Formula Ford with a few distinguished results, a first place at Lydden Hill in May being the highlight, but he also distinguished himself off the track in the way only he could at times. At Vallelunga in Italy he was due to compete in the European Formula Ford Championship, and after travelling across countries to get there, he was informed that his medical certificate was not valid as his blood group was not recorded. This infuriated Hunt, who genuinely believed the regulations hadn't stated this, and in protest drove his car to the front of the grid, parked it at a ninety degree angle and walked away, so delaying the start. For him it was another way, albeit childishly, of making a statement. Unfortunately for him it was witnessed by Stuart Turner of the Ford Motor Company who was spectating from the grandstand. Legend has it that he turned to his colleague, the later esteemed journalist Nick Brittan and said: 'Mark my words, that young man is going nowhere in motor racing' For his part, Brittan took James to one side and remarked: 'You'll never make a professional racing driver as long as you've got a hole in your arse'. Two prophecies that were somewhat wide of the mark. James was undaunted and by the end of the year he too had graduated to the Grand Prix stepping-stone that was Formula Three.

CHAPTER FOUR

Formula Three, the stepping stone

Hunt's break into Formula Three came with Motor Racing Enterprises, a team that ran Brabhams. His earlier Formula Ford victory at Lydden Hill had been in one of their cars when he'd been asked to replace their driver, and so impressed were they that it seemed a natural progression to move up the ladder and compete in the fiercely competitive Formula Three category. He finished seventh on his debut at Mallory Park in August and found himself competing against some of the great future names of the sport in Fittipaldi, Peterson, Laffite and Jarier. The grids were huge and the standards very high, yet Hunt's persistence paid dividends, coupled with a talent that was now being recognised, it meant he was seen in a serious light by the racing fraternity.

A well-earned fourth place at the spectacularly scenic Caldwell Park circuit in September, where he finished a fraction of a second behind the star-of-the-moment Ronnie Peterson after a race-long duel, prompted the March team to offer him a drive – ironically replacing the injured Peterson in the next race in France. Although he struggled to settle with the new car, and finished a lowly tenth, the fact that teams were approaching him was again proof that James Hunt was on his way.

Hunt leads Peterson for 3rd place at Caldwell Park

Also proof was a second place at the end-of-year Grovewood Awards, selected by a panel of the British Guild of Motoring Writers, as one of the most promising drivers in the country. First place went to the F5000 driver Mike Walker, but James was sufficiently impressed enough to wear a suit and tie for the occasion at the Royal Automobile Club in London, something he had failed to do the last time he'd been invited and had been refused entry! A cheque of £300 made up for any discomfort he must have been feeling, and that money went some way to paying off numerous debts, with the Award helping when he did the rounds of door-knocking with potential sponsors. At the end of 1969, James Hunt was the 'coming man' of British motor racing.

Sadly, no matter how great the talent, no matter how committed the man, if the funds aren't there, then it will be a struggle, and for James Hunt 1970 was indeed a struggle. Not necessarily on the track, where he excelled in the car, a recently bought Lotus 59 with financial help from Molyslip, but off the track where finances were at times beyond the critical stage. His deal with Lotus meant the provision of the car and repairs, plus around £1,000 for travel and expenses, but as Hunt was travelling all over the Continent to compete, he was relying heavily on prize funds to keep him afloat. That meant living in a tent and forgoing any kind of social life whatsoever, something which must have been almost purgatory for a man so inclined as Hunt. At times the critical stage went beyond and crashing his Lotus a couple of times in qualifying meant that there was no time for a repair and so no start and in turn no starting money. In fact his financial state was so bad that one evening he could be seen siphoning petrol from a competitor, unbeknown to the man himself, so as to have enough to drive back to the ferry at Le Havre. It also meant no food for two days.

On the track though, he continued to impress, if not at times in a rather cavalier fashion. His first visit to the glamour that was Monaco ended in an accident, and it is fair to say the principality was never to his liking and in years to come actually heralded his farewell from the sport, but there were some very notable performances. After an arduous journey through the Austrian Alps, not helped by over-officious Italian custom officials (more of them later!), he managed a creditable second at the wonderful Osterreichring. A couple more second places followed, including one in Belgium where he spun from the lead on the penultimate lap and then managed to overtake four cars on the last lap only to be out-dragged to the finishing line.

His first victory of the season came at Rouen in France where after a frenetic race of slip streaming and last ditch overtaking, he pipped Wilson Fittipaldi and Mike Beuttler to the chequered flag. Unfortunately the race was overshadowed by serious injuries to French drivers Denis Dayan and Bob Wolleck and the death of another, Jean-Luc Salomon, after a last lap overtaking manoeuvre had gone horribly wrong.

In the 1970s this was part of motor racing. Safety was a passing diversion and it wasn't until Jackie Stewart, who was World Champion at that time, really put his heart and soul into making the sport safer, that the number of fatalities per season rapidly reduced. Stewart was almost singularly instrumental in changing the face of the sport, despite opposition from circuit owners and at times his fellow drivers, and it is fair to say that many lives have been saved due to his tireless work.

If the danger posed a problem for Hunt, then he had no shame in admitting it. His pre-race ritual of vomiting, no matter where he was or who he was with, became a feature of his build-up. There was no sense of embarrassment, as that particular trait seemed to have deserted him at an early age, and the nerves he showed before the start of a race could be quite disconcerting as it seemed to the outsider that he was a bundle of energy that needed harnessing. It never changed throughout his career.

That bundle of energy had to be dispersed somehow and of course racing a car at very fast speeds was the ideal way, but if something was to interrupt that, then all hell would break loose. This was perfectly illustrated at Crystal Palace in October 1970 towards the end of the Formula Three season that had seen Hunt reasonably successful with a couple of victories at Rouen and Zolder, plus numerous high-placings. He was certainly one of the men to beat and as the race was being televised live by the BBC, a rare event in those days, everyone was out to impress. Hunt had finished second in the qualifying heat and in the final he was battling for second place with Mike Beuttler and David Morgan. On the last lap, as Australian Dave Walker took the chequered flag, Hunt and Morgan collided in spectacular fashion with Morgan's March thumping into the safety barrier and Hunt's Lotus skidding to a halt in the centre of the track, minus two wheels. The screaming pack of cars that followed tried to take emergency evasive action, while Hunt climbed out of the cockpit, ran to Morgan and promptly flattened him with a blow to the head. It was all caught live in front of an astonished television audience and the resulting furore saw James Hunt's image battered in the aftermath. He was castigated by the motor racing fraternity in the specialised press, yet when the incident was brought to a Royal Automobile Club Tribunal, it was Morgan who received the severe punishment of a twelve month suspension on his racing licence. James Hunt had gathered a number of witnesses, drivers included, plus video tape of the live coverage to prove that Morgan had overtaken him in a dangerous manner. It seemed to many that Morgan had been made a scapegoat and a year later he got his licence back and continued his racing career, never really to bother anyone again. The same could not be said about James Hunt.

At the tribunal, and attending on James's behalf, was John Hogan. He was working for an advertising company and Hunt had asked him for advice on how to get sponsorship. Hogan helped him to contact Coca-Cola, but became a very important member of the James Hunt team in years to come and would help him become the World Champion he'd predicted when he first started racing.

For Niki Lauda, 1970 was one of those 'learning' years which as time passes seem to gain a more romantic edge to the way it was perceived at that moment. He was hugely in debt and spent virtually the whole year travelling around the Continent competing in various Formula Three events, with little success. His first race had seen him travel for thirty-six hours to Nogaro in the South of France with another Austrian driver to compete against, as he called them: 'thirty mad Frenchmen'. The race lasted five minutes for Lauda as he and his compatriot Gerold Pankl somehow contrived to have an accident together and Lauda's car ended up ploughing through the guard-rail, destroying itself in the process. A first taste of Formula Three and a sour one at that.

More debt followed as he drove to Germany to buy a new car. With that he drove to the Nurburgring circuit and whilst in fifth place spun out without anyone remotely close to him on the track. Another one and a half day drive to France again, another race and this time the gearbox breaks on him. It was becoming, even at that early stage of the season, quite disheartening and only his fortitude and sheer bloody-mindedness kept him going plus the need for prize money to pay off his accumulating debts!

At Brands Hatch, a photographer called Alois Rottensteiner asked him where the best place would be to get the most spectacular photographs, so Lauda told him to position himself: 'Just ahead of the pits, somebody's bound to lose it there'. Lauda promptly did just that after a risky overtaking manoeuvre and again another complete car write-off. At least Rottensteiner got his picture.

At the time Lauda was occasionally racing against Hunt, but there was nothing but a passing interest from both of them, and it is fair to say that if someone was able to predict the more successful of the two in the future, it would surely have been the Englishman. Lauda was fast, but crashed a lot. More than Hunt in fact, who had the 'Shunt' title attached to him wherever he went. The Austrian paid no heed to such things until a particularly bad accident towards the end of the year at Zolder, the race that saw James Hunt take his second victory of the season. On lap three, as he was in a maelstrom of weaving and bobbing racing cars, they crested a brow only to come across an ambulance travelling at 30mph attending an accident. Most of the cars somehow managed to squeeze through the ever-diminishing gap, but one of them didn't. After colliding with another, Lauda was sat in his cockpit waiting for the next melee of screaming cars to converge on the scene. One literally ran over the nose of his and with that Niki extricated himself from the stricken vehicle and ran off. It was at that stage that he had a defining moment. From that point he would analyse everything about the sport and reduce the risks drastically.

The season ended for him with a few Sportscar races, mainly to pay off some of his debts, and he had quite a bit of success, notably in a round of the World Championship in Austria where he was placed sixth. He won a few minor events, but it was clear his future lay in single-seaters. This was despite the disastrous year he'd experienced and the fact that the great Jochen Rindt, his fellow countryman, had been killed at the Italian Grand Prix in September. Lauda's single resolve was to continue and he decided that 1971 would be a step up to Formula Two, and of course another heavy debt that would inevitably follow.

CHAPTER FIVE

Lauda pays his way

Paying for a drive in any formula in motor racing is now an accepted part of making progress, but in the early 1970s it was virtually unheard of. With the advent of sponsorship, particularly in the highest sphere, money became more and more important, and for the teams who were struggling, a driver who could combine a turn of speed and invest a healthy financial amount would be preferred. It was that combination that brought Niki Lauda to the March team. They had been founded two years previously with Max Mosley amongst the men in charge and it was he who Lauda approached about the possibility of partnering the super-fast Ronnie Peterson for the following season. Mosley took to the aristocratic Lauda name, something which his background had appreciated, and agreed that Niki could drive in Formula Two in 1971, but it would cost around one million schillings. Lauda didn't baulk at the figure and immediately contacted a leading Austrian bank 'Erste Oesterreichische Spar-Casse' and arranged an advertising deal. Suffice to say that the Lauda family name was of no hindrance in this matter.

As his debt became higher, so his stock amongst the motor racing fraternity receded as in the 1971 season Lauda was simply out-classed by his more experienced team-mate. In fourteen races he managed a high of just fourth place whilst Peterson took the European crown and on only one occasion did he get the better of the blonde Swede, even then he was told by his team to back off as all of their efforts were concentrated on getting Peterson to the front. He competed in a few sportscar events and managed a victory at the Salzburgring, but it hardly registered on the radar of potential team managers and sponsors. Lauda was just another driver who had ambition, but seemingly only a modicum of talent.

Amazingly, just three years after starting in the sport, he started a Formula One Grand Prix. It was at the Oesterreichring for the 1971 Austrian Grand Prix and after paying to use the March 711, he qualified second last on the grid for his home race and after twenty laps brought it into the pits declaring the car 'undriveable'. It was an inauspicious start to his F1 career and especially as the very same car driven by the ever-impressive Peterson finished second in that year's World Championship behind Jackie Stewart. Lauda had inner doubts about his ability, but his partner Mariella, who travelled everywhere with him as he chased his fading dream, kept faith in his ability and it was decided that for the next year he would take the almost unprecedented step of borrowing yet more money and buy into the March Formula One set-up for 1972. To say Niki was determined is an understatement of massive proportions as it is fair to say there would not be a single team manager on the grid who would give a momentary second's thought to hiring him as a number one driver.

The amount required was monumental, at least five times more than he paid in 1971, but again he approached the bank and they were agreeable, only for the deal to fall through after an untimely call from 'Old Lauda', Niki's now nemesis grandfather. He had called an end to the transaction through his association with the bank to 'bring the lad to his senses' and the two never spoke again.

Lauda, never one to shy away from a challenge, then contacted a second bank and set up a line of credit to pay for the season. It was risky of course but he just got on with it and allowed the money problems to take care of themselves. One thing the young man didn't appreciate at the time though was that the March team were experiencing a certain amount of financial difficulty despite their high profile few years, and Lauda's money effectively saved the team for that season. It was obviously a partnership made to survive.

1972 was a combination of F1 and F2 races for both team and drivers, with again Peterson leading from the front and Lauda trying in desperation to hang on. The first two Grands Prix in Argentina and South Africa saw him finish, but well out of the points and all hopes were on the new car that would be available for Spain. It was a complete disaster and after a couple more races, in which again the Super-Swede completely out-performed Lauda, the car was scrapped. In a way it helped him assuage his inner doubts as after finding it difficult to drive, he had spoken to the technicians who had initially dismissed his concerns, only to eventually agree that he was right all along and that the car was frankly awful. It was a small defining moment for the Austrian as it proved that, although he was without the raw speed that was needed at that stage, he certainly understood what made a racing car tick.

Lauda in the paid-for March 722 at Rouen

Formula Two was proving some solace for Lauda, as at one stage he led the Championship, but familiar mechanical problems caused his demise and by October the situation was dire. The ever popular Ronne Peterson had left March for Lotus and the team had decided that Lauda was only Formula Two material from now on. Add that to his now crippling debts, which were close to bankrupting him, and for the first and only time in his life he actually had suicidal thoughts. As he said: 'When I drove away from Bicester after a final confrontation with March, the thought went through my head that I could end it there and then'. Thankfully he didn't and as life has always a way of producing a surprise, he was soon contacted by an elder statesman of the sport Louis Stanley, the boss of the famous BRM team. Just when there seemed to be no hope, then it arrived in an unlikely form.

CHAPTER SIX

James lags behind

Whilst Niki Lauda was forging an initially unsuccessful Formula One career, James Hunt was still struggling in Formula Three, yet briefly in 1971 they actually shared a flat together in West London. As the lifestyle that James enjoyed probably meant a flat full of drinking buddies and alcohol-fuelled parties with numerous women, 'sharing' was something of a mis-nomer. Lauda never embraced that type of living, although he remembered James as an 'open, honest-to-God pal'. He also came out with the famous quote that he enjoyed sex as much as the next man, 'unless that man was James Hunt'.

On the track, Hunt reasoned that another season in Formula Three would sharpen the edges of his driving and would then lead to a direct route to Formula One. He was given a works drive with March and with sponsor-ship from Coca-Cola actually started to enjoy a more civilised life, staying in hotels instead of tents, as he toured the Continent in search of success. That came, with victories in France, Germany and two in the UK, but it was the year that the 'Hunt the Shunt' title really stuck. He seemed to crash just about everywhere and from every conceivable position too.

At Pau he went off on the first lap, then at Silverstone he waited until the last lap before flying off in spectacular fashion, but it was at Zandvoort in Holland that he really excelled. He'd qualified at the back of the grid due to engine problems and had attempted to make up for it by scything his way through the field, but on the eleventh lap he made contact with another car at the notoriously difficult Tarzan corner. Hunt's car flipped upside down, the roll-bar snapping off in the process, and then skated for a hundred yards before hitting the fencing. Somehow he extricated himself from the car that was in danger of bursting into flames and sat ashen-faced at the side of the track nursing a damaged vertebrae, torn back muscles and serious bruising.

In fact this had been a rather traumatic weekend for the playboy racer, as the night before he had attempted to treat an 'intimate' area of his body that was suffering from a well known affliction with undiluted lotion and severely burnt himself. The agony that ensued was heard all around the hotel!

James was living life to the full on and off the track. On it, the accident had started to register and it was at this time that he remembered having a long talk with Niki about the dangers they faced each time they climbed into the cockpit. They both agreed that it was the life they had chosen, so they may as well have as much fun as they could whilst it lasted. James of course was able to take that to the ultimate degree.

By now his relationship with 'Ping' had faltered and his dalliances with other women just increased. He spent a few months with a French girl called Michelle, then immediately met a Belgian lady, Chantal, who he moved in with, yet the commitment was fragile at best. Most nights, when he wasn't travelling to and from racing circuits, he could be seen in the local hostelries in west London, drinking and chatting up waitresses. He seemed to have a pop star aura about him in that small bubble that he inhabited and his racing escapades became stories that would become more and more exaggerated as the evenings wore on. To be fair to James though, he was disciplined with his drinking as a race weekend approached, refusing anything alcoholic from Wednesday onwards so he could be in peak condition for the weekend.

His recovery from the accident was slow and the rest of the season saw him continue to make an impact with either stunning front position drives or jaw-dropping accidents. Another big accident at Snetterton saw him injure his shoulder and arm, but he still continued to record good results, and even found himself competing in a Formula Two race in late summer. Alongside Formula One drivers Graham Hill, Emerson Fittipaldi and Ronnie Peterson, he acquitted himself quite well and finished a respectable twelfth.

At the end of the year Hunt had showed the extremes of his talent and enthusiasm with victories and crashes in equal measure. The Autosport journalist Ian Phillips said of him: 'I actually believed in the guy, but it was bloody difficult to justify sometimes. Unfortunately his hot-headedness sometimes betrayed his sense of responsibility.' As for the 'Hunt the Shunt' title, James shrugged it off, believing that it was an easy rhyme and didn't mean anything. It was true that he did mangle his car a few too many times, but that was Formula Three in the early 70s.

The next season was simply a 'make-or-break' one for James. He had watched as his friend Lauda had somehow managed to get himself in Formula One, despite having a less impressive record than him and also after numerous more accidents than him, and here he was starting out for another campaign in Formula Three. Of course he needed money, and he came up with his ingenious idea of approaching his Grandmother for the inheritance he would receive from her will, but before she died! In fact, he approached his parents with the idea, but it didn't find favour unsurprisingly.

He signed again for the March team, but the season was a disaster, actually described by Autosport magazine as 'shambolic'. The car was woefully uncompetitive and among the usual spate of accidents, Hunt struggled to finish higher than third all season. It then became obvious that the March team were in serious financial difficulties, as had been suggested with Niki Lauda, and there were fears that Hunt would be dropped for the German Jochen Mass, who was bringing the might of the Ford Company of Germany with him. At Monaco the car failed to appear for practice, much to Hunt's anger, and when it finally did it was in no state to race. Hunt, by now paranoid over his placing in the team, made the incredible decision to race for his ex-manager Chris Marshall in a privately-owned March. That brought about an ultimatum from team owner Max Mosley telling him to either race the ill-prepared car or be dismissed with immediate effect. Hunt decided to continue to race the private car and promptly crashed it into the barrier. He was then sacked by March.

One more race followed and then it was over. Hunt was without a drive as Marshall's regular driver had returned and James faced an as-usual uncertain future. He was advised to forget about racing for the rest of the year, get a job and spend the time seeking sponsorship. That was never likely to happen and so another plan was needed. It came in the rather odd surroundings of a cow pasture in Belgium.

CHAPTER SEVEN

Hesketh, 'Bubbles' and the Playboy

Lord Alexander Hesketh was one of the richest men in the country and at the age of 22 owned the racing team 'Hesketh Racing'. He had inherited his father's wealth, which included the estate of Easton Neston, 9,000 acres of farmland and the Towcester racecourse. He wore a Rolex watch and his personal transport included a Jet Ranger helicopter, a Porsche, a Mercedes and a chauffer-driven Rolls-Royce with in-built telephone system, something unheard of in the 1970s. He was a portly figure who enjoyed the best cigars, champagne and numerous female companions, but he also had an incredibly low boredom threshold.

Anthony Horsley, or 'Bubbles' as he was affectionately known (coming about after buying a racing car owned by lady racer Bluebell Gibbs. He took on her name and then somehow it was changed to Bubbles by an acquaintance, the great F1 driver Piers Courage), was motor-trader-cum-racing-driver-cum-actor and spent most of his early years wheeling and dealing his way across the Continent. He'd met Hesketh at a wedding and tried to sell him a car, but after a riotous evening ended up buying one from him instead! They became great friends and when Hesketh decided to start up a racing team, 'Bubbles' became driver and team manager all-in-one.

The meeting in the cow pasture in Chimay, Belgium was actually on the 21st May 1972 when Hunt went looking for a benefactor and had heard of the new Hesketh team who were looking for a competitive driver. 'Bubbles' was also looking for James as he'd watched Hunt finish fifth that afternoon and realised immediately that he could do more justice to their car than he ever could. 'We sort of found each other. We needed each other. It was a marriage of convenience.' Horsley would later say, yet Lord Hesketh's initial impressions of Hunt were not as favourable. The fact that the introduction took place in an army tent that doubled as a toilet was hardly inspiring, but Hesketh's comment that Hunt seemed 'rather pleased with himself' was not exactly promising. However, a deal was struck and James Hunt became the sole driver for the Hesketh Racing Team from that point on.

If Hesketh had any misgivings at the time, they were multiplied after their first races together at Silverstone. For the first time a Hesketh car was leading, but sadly for them it was travelling backwards, as in the wet Hunt had spun and planted the car against the pit-wall immediately in front of his new boss.

The next race at Brands Hatch saw Hunt destroy the Hesketh Formula Three team.

In the Dastle car that they were running, he was close behind another when a deflating tyre caused it to slow. Hunt tried to take avoiding action, but only succeeded in cartwheeling after contact and a terrifying series of rolls saw the car destroy itself and land upside down astride a crash barrier. After righting itself, James could be seen pushing the start button frantically and screaming at the lack of response. As the engine was on the other side of the track, it was a futile exercise.

Somehow his weekend got worse. The race was a support for the British Grand Prix, and James had decided to watch the beginning and then leave early to avoid the traffic and watch the end on television. With girlfriend Chantal and close friend Brendan McInerney, he set off in his Mini at great speed and immediately encountered a Volvo on the wrong side of the road. The head on collision was followed by a huge impact with a tree, causing four of Chantal's ribs to be broken and serious leg injuries to James. Despite his self-remedy of a pint of beer at the close-by pub, he was hospitalised for a week, but was quickly discharged after being caught with a female in a compromising position by the matron. For James Hunt this was just another weekend of his life.

By now Lord Hesketh was seriously unimpressed with both James Hunt and the Formula Three scene, especially after an argument with the Brands Hatch officials as to where he could park his helicopter. Hunt was also unimpressed with F3 and decided he needed to progress to Formula Two and came across a great idea. He composed a letter threatening to sue Max Mosley for his dismissal, but would agree to waive it if Mosley would supply an F2 chassis on loan. Amazingly the scheme worked and after Hesketh bought an engine and painted the car with 'Hesketh Racing' on the side, they entered the Rothmans 5000 race at Brands Hatch in August. It was an event for F1, F2, F5000 and sports cars combined and James finished a creditable fifth behind the current leader of the World Championship Emerson Fittipaldi.

Despite still healing from his injuries, James went from strength to strength, actually finishing on the podium at Oulton Park after a great scrap between himself, Ronnie Peterson and Niki Lauda, two drivers who were enjoying far more success than he. The third place actually came after an excursion off circuit through the undergrowth and weeds and it was this performance that redeemed him in the eyes of Lord Hesketh. Although he'd missed the race for a shooting weekend, the reports he'd received convinced him that he should re-organise the team and prepare for a full-on assault on Formula Two in 1973. They even travelled to Brazil at the end of the season to compete in two races where James hardly impressed, but certainly enjoyed the lifestyle. Some of the pranks that were recorded and witnessed would be etched in the minds of everyone for the rest of their lives and one female member was so outraged that she screamed that she and her husband would ensure that James Hunt would never, ever get into Formula One. Within a few months, he was there.

The Hesketh team announced at the beginning of the year that they would not only compete in Formula Two, but at some stage during the season, they would try their hand at Formula One. This was greeted with barely suppressed smirks by the motor sport establishment, and Hesketh's cause was hardly helped by Hunt breaking his arm whilst 'playing silly games' on the lawn after having lunch in the country. His reputation wasn't exactly in tatters as he wasn't regarded that highly anyway, but none of it helped.

Hesketh were also looked upon with a degree of suspicion when they decided to change the face of motor racing by turning up at circuits wearing a red, white and blue uniform, in deference to the Union Flag. This was unusual to say the least, as in the past most participants had embraced the grease and dirt that was usually associated with anything to do with the combustion engine. Mechanics had to be grubby right?

Alongside this show of new-professionalism there was the show of opulence with helicopters carrying the huge entourage who came along just to enjoy the vast hospitality laid on by Lord Hesketh. Frankly the sport had never seen anything quite like it, and although the grandeur and glamour that is Formula One today is almost taken for granted, in the 1970s it was as uncommon as seeing an alien walking down the High Street.

Underneath the party-atmosphere, there was a serious side and after failing in an F2 event, Hunt was entered for the 'Race of Champions' at Brands Hatch his Formula One debut. Amazingly, he qualified 13th in a car that he admitted was driving him due to the extra power, but in front of nearly 50,000 delirious fans, actually came third! It was the moment that James Hunt was finally taken seriously. It also saw the once-ridiculed Hesketh team become a little more important, although their F2 dalliances saw little success as mishap and ill-luck followed them, from Thruxton in southern England, to Pau in France. Not to be disheartened by any of it though, James whose arm was now healed completely, entertained Miss Pau for the weekend and the arm found itself linked with the beauty queen for the duration.

It became clear to Lord Hesketh that F2 was a waste of his time and he made the rather obvious decision to move up to Formula One. He reasoned that the team may as well be at the back of the grid in Grand Prix racing as opposed to Formula Two and have more fun doing it! So Monaco saw the official arrival of the Hesketh Racing Formula One Team and there could not have been a more apt place to start.

Monaco is glamour. There is no other word to describe it, yet in the 1970s that glamour comprised a few millionaires with small sailing boats bobbing around in the harbour. There were expensive cars, champagne and cigars with exotic women aplenty, but nothing could really prepare for the impact that the Hesketh team had on the principality that June 1973. The 'Southern Breeze' was probably the largest yacht there, with the Bell Jet Ranger helicopter parked alongside for good measure. On the harbour front a Rolls-Royce Corniche, a Porsche Carrera and a new range Suzuki motorcycle stood awaiting, whilst the best food and drink was served by scantily clad ladies. Pete Lyons of Autosport loved it and said it would stir up the rather staid F1 circus, but the team that lavished money on the trappings of the scene and called each other 'Le Patron' (Hesketh), 'Bubbles' (Horsley) and 'Superstar' (Hunt), and would gather together to pray to the 'great chicken in the sky' for good weather and numerous other benefits, were actually ready to take on the Grand Prix grid.

Hunt and Hesketh at Monaco, never a happy hunting-ground

A new March731 had been purchased off Max Mosley and Dr Harvey Postlethwaite, later to become one of the sport's most admired engineers was recruited. James qualified 18th amongst the great names of the sport, Hulme, Stewart, Peterson, Fittipaldi and Cevert, promptly threw up before the race in his usual ritual and blew his engine on the 73rd lap whilst running ninth. It was an inauspicious start but it showed Hunt how super-fit he had to be to compete as he admitted afterwards that he was white-faced with exhaustion and trembling from the effort of driving a 500 horsepower car that had mini-mal safety measures surrounding the 40 gallon fuel tank.

One month later, in France and in only his second Grand Prix, Hunt scored his first World Championship point by finishing sixth. An incredible achieve-ment and finally the title of 'Hunt the Shunt' was being forgotten. Hesketh was partying as if there was no tomorrow, but on the track they were upset-ting the establishment just as forcibly. He came fourth at the British Grand Prix at Silverstone (a race noted for one of the biggest crashes in the history of the sport when Jody Scheckter's McLaren triggered an accident at Woodcote that nearly wiped out the entire field) where Jackie Stewart struggled down in tenth. There was a new hero for the British public to cheer on and the pop star looks that James had, endeared him to a new army of fans. He was the devil-may-care to Stewart's conservatism even if Stewart did have his own film star looks and his aura was one of fun and excitement. He was the new pin-up boy of F1 who lived the life it brought to the maximum.

Two weeks later he finished third at the Dutch Grand Prix, but the race will always be remembered for the terrible accident that cost the life of Roger Williamson. Watched by millions live on television, his upturned car burnt with the British driver trapped inside as fellow driver David Purley tried in vain to help. The images were horrific as other cars sped by and the woefully inadequate safety marshalls stood and stared as a man's life ebbed away. It was this, at a circuit that had implemented all the latest safety features in a bid to get a long term contract for Grand Prix racing, that finally persuaded the ambivalent amongst the F1 fraternity that Jackie Stewart's safety campaign had merit after all.

James was affected by the accident as he knew Williamson well, so in a way of blocking it out of his mind he threw himself into as many other types of racing as he could, such as sportscars and CanAm racing. He also returned to the Zandvoort circuit two weeks later to compete in a saloon car event, but F1 was the priority. Austria and Italy were anti-climaxes, especially at Monza where he failed to qualify after crashing. This brought about one of the typical James rages as he blamed everyone for the failure, right down to 'Bubbles' for not flying out a new chassis in time for the race. His anger was well known around the team, but as a man who lived on his emotions, it was indulged as opposed to discouraged.

The season ended with an excellent second place at the United States Grand Prix at Watkins Glen in New York where he harried the eventual winner Ronnie Peterson, finishing just 0.688 seconds behind. Sadly again, any pleasure in the podium was tempered by yet more tragic news. Francois Cevert was killed when his Tyrrell hit two barriers and was sliced in half. A driver of incredible talent, he was a future World Champion without any doubt, and his team mate Jackie Stewart, who had just won the Championship for a third time and had already decided to retire, quit with immediate effect. It was yet another terrible reminder that motor racing in the 1970s was as close to suicide as you could get, unless you were very, very lucky.

When the team returned they announced a full blown attack on the 1974 season with an increased budget of £200,000 (they had spent around £68,000 in 1973) and for good measure Hunt, who had finished eighth in the standings with 14 points, was awarded the Campbell Trophy by the RAC for the best performance in motor sport by a British driver in a British car, eclipsing even Stewart and the essentially British Tyrrell team. Hunt and Hesketh had arrived.

CHAPTER EIGHT

Wheeling and Dealing Lauda

Niki Lauda's arrival at the once-successful BRM team was as fortuitous as it was necessary for both sides. Lauda was without a drive with nowhere to go in Formula One and BRM were simply without money after their main sponsor, Marlboro, threatened to withdraw. BRM had been a very capable team and had taken Graham Hill to the World Championship in 1962, but as the years passed the force had declined and in the hands of Louis Stanley, the son-in-law of the original owner Lord Alfred Owen, they were simply a shadow of themselves, despite the talents of Clay Regazzoni, Vern Schuppan and Jean-Pierre Beltoise as their drivers. The two met at Vienna airport and after Stanley calmly informed Lauda that he could only offer a pay-per-drive to the Austrian, Niki did what he had become good at. He went into more debt!

In what was a mind-boggling scheme, Lauda convinced his new owner-prospect that the bank would pay the two million schillings required, with the first third paid when Stanley released the starting-money from his first race. Lauda's plan included racing in as many saloon car events as possible to help pay the debt, and with that sense of total self-belief Niki carried on his racing career as his debt mounted to such a degree that it could easily be mistaken for the annual income of a developing-world country.

The car, despite its pole position at the first race of the season with Regazzoni, was disastrously inadequate. It broke down on numerous occasions when it wasn't being outclassed. The team were simply not able to develop it due to the severe financial restraints, and Stanley played the part of the perfect English gentleman to a tee as he toured the World in charge of a professional racing team. Sadly he was not able to play the part of a team owner/manager as there was no direction or guidance and it became quite simply a rudderless ship. Despite this, Niki managed to score his first points with a fifth place at Zolder in Belgium. In fact his performances, which far outweighed anything the cumbersome red and white machine could manage, were attracting the attentions of many.

By the time the circus had arrived in Monaco, a certain Enzo Ferrari was showing a more than keen interest in the young Austrian. With his single-seater performances at Grands Prix, plus numerous successes in saloon cars, his talent was now burgeoning. His finances were as critical as ever, so it must have been an incredible moment when he was told by Stanley that he would now be employed as a pay driver on a two year contract. For the first time, he was being paid as opposed to paying for his career. What he didn't know at that time, was that Stanley had got wind of Ferrari's interest and made a point of tying him down.

Lauda at Monaco, already Ferrari were admirers

The team lurched from one crisis to another. Tired of driving a car that relied on second hand parts, Regazzoni walked out and joined Ferrari and immediately told Enzo that his team-mate should be Niki. The Old Man had lost Jacky Ickx and dismissed Arturio Merzario in a desperate attempt to win a World Championship that had eluded them since 1964. He paid off Lauda's contract at BRM (not difficult as Louis Stanley had 'forgotten' to pay him his starting money), plus all of his debts and loans, and with that Niki Lauda swopped what he described as a group of kite enthusiasts for a position at

NASA. The change was that dramatic. From a team that was still using old parts that they couldn't afford to replace and certainly living on its former glories in the shape of Hawthorn, Hill, Moss, Behra etc, to another team that too had former glories, but had the resources to climb back to the top.

Lauda hardly gave a backward glance at BRM and was upset that there had been no words of good luck from its eccentric owner, but three years later, Stanley proved the gentleman he was by arranging a leading British surgeon to help Niki's recovery after his dreadful Nurburgring accident. More of that to come.

The set-up at the Fiorano-based team was incredible. It had its own private test track, the best engineers and mechanics and a culture and history that almost transcended the sport. All it needed now was success, and Lauda free from any financial concerns was the man who was destined to bring it back. It had been a remarkable rise for the Viennese driver who had been forced to literally pay his way into the sport. 1974 was the year that Niki Lauda as a racing driver finally came into his own and the legend that lives today was first forged. Ferrari and Lauda was a match made in heaven and later a nightmare cast in hell.

The name of Ferrari is sacrosanct in Formula One. Without it, then it is fair to say the sport would not exist in its current form. Ferrari has for many years been the driving force and the team that almost every driver without exception has wanted to join, yet in the early 1970s 'the prancing horse' was in complete disarray. They hadn't won a title since 1964 and on regular occasions even failed to qualify for Grands Prix. The team that Lauda joined was a complete mess with a car that was uncompetitive and alarmingly slow, the blame always laid fairly and squarely on the shoulders of the drivers. One thing that Old Man Ferrari would not do would be to criticise or even believe that his cars were not up to the job. It would always be the drivers, and as in his eccentricity he never, ever attended a race, or indeed left his Maranello home, then what was told him by the minions who were employed, would be the truth he always wanted to hear. The cars were fine it was just the drivers!

Jacky Ickx and Arturio Merzario had been released and Lauda and Regazzoni were the latest protagonists to attempt to turn around the great team's fortunes. Lauda immediately decided that the best form of defence was to attack, and in a meeting with Mr Ferrari (through an interpreter Piero Lardi, an illegitimate son of the Old Man who was not allowed to use the surname for many years – and was reluctant to translate completely), Lauda told him that his car was awful and it needed fixing. In turn Ferrari told him he had to be one second faster within a week otherwise he would be out! Thankfully the great engineer Mauro Forghieri had been called back to work on the recalcitrant cars, and that extra speed was attained.

The season started off well with a first podium finish for second place in Argentina. He got on well with 'Regga', a man who was relaxed in and out of the car and loved to enjoy life to the full. A serial womaniser who had more in common with James Hunt than Niki Lauda, but the two of them complimented each other perfectly. With the help of another Ferrari 'great', team manager Luca Montezemolo, Niki actually won two Grands Prix in 1974. The first was at Jarama in Spain, where after starting on pole, he mastered the changing conditions and recorded the first victory for a scarlet car for two years, and then later in the season he did the same at Zandvoort in Holland to briefly take the lead in the World Championship. Niki was the 'flavour of the month', yet it is interesting that in his excellent biography 'To Hell and Back' written in 1986, both races are hardly referred to. For a man who was destined to give the famous team its greatest success for years, it is amazing that it seemed to be but a footnote in his own personal history.

Lauda was now in demand and as he worked for an Italian team with the media following his every move, he decided to learn the language too. It was also a way of listening to what the mechanics were saying about him as well! Sadly his Championship challenge faded away as the season progressed following a series of retirements and at the last Grand Prix of the campaign, at Watkins Glen in the US, it was his team-mate Regazzoni who was head-to-head with Emerson Fittipaldi in the McLaren for the title. Despite Lauda's efforts to help his friend, it was the Brazilian who recorded his second World Title, on a day when Austrian Helmut Koenigg in only his second Grand Prix-was killed after hitting a barrier on the tenth lap.

The season had been a success for Lauda though and the trappings and remuneration were certainly affecting his life. He took flying lessons and bought himself a Cessna Golden Eagle, firstly for purely practical reasons with the amount of travelling involved, and then for passionate reasons as it became an interest that would then stay with him for the rest of his life. He was adored in his home country of Austria where he was simply referred to as Niki, in Italy due to his connection with Ferrari, and rather oddly in Germany too. Sadly his personal life had started to unravel with Mariella. They were due to move out of their apartment in Salzburg and had decided to build a house in another area, but in the summer of 1975 he met Marlene Knaus at a party held by her boyfriend Curd Jurgens. They bonded almost immediately, and in what could be described as unseemly haste, they dated and Lauda left Mariella, whilst Marlene said goodbye to Jurgens. It soon became public knowledge and for a while they were the subject of intense scrutiny in Austria, and indeed in certain parts of the world where his name meant something. By 1976 they were married and neither looked back. Thankfully for the two of them, the controversy and scandal that had attached to them was somewhat overshadowed by James Hunt inevitably, with the breakdown of his marriage to Suzy Miller in 1976 and her affair with actor Richard Burton. Not for the first time was Lauda relieved that his lifestyle was the antithesis of his great friend. Whilst Hunt surrounded himself with as many acolytes and 'hangers-on' as he could and spent most of his days womanising and cramming as much fun into each and every day, Niki preferred to have all but the closest friends in his entourage, eating at local restaurants and living a far simpler lifestyle. Good but opposite friends.

CHAPTER NINE

The Playboy gets serious

James Hunt's retainer was increased to £15,000 for 1974, a clear indication that the Hesketh team were attacking Formula One in a serious way. Their budget was around £200,000 and at the beginning of the year the new car, the 308, was wheeled out to the waiting media. Whilst not having the stunning good looks of later F1 models, it was a purposeful beast and looked the part. It was devoid of any sponsorship whatsoever as Lord Hesketh thought that too vulgar and its virginal white colour with red and blue stripes gave it the patriotic feeling that British enthusiasts could identify with. The team even printed a glossy booklet called 'The Heavily Censored History of Hesketh Racing' for their new legion of fans, but it was a tongue-in-cheek way of raising a little more cash and direct them to the various merchandise that could be purchased.

For the opening two races of the season in Argentina and Brazil the team stayed faithful to the 'old' car, the March731 and it nearly paid off. Hunt qualified fifth in Argentina (taking great delight in walking to the Ferrari pit and teasing Lauda about being ahead of him) and actually took the lead on the opening lap! Sadly his enthusiasm got the better of him and after passing Ronnie Peterson he immediately slithered off the circuit damaging the car. After a trip to the pits to repair any damage, he retired with an overheating engine. To say that 'Bubbles' was unimpressed with Hunt's cavalier driving was something of an understatement as he had thrown away their first ever lead! The threat of the sack seemed to be a calming influence.

Brazil was uneventful on the track with a ninth place, but with a £7,000 'recreational' advance to spend, Hunt and the team enjoyed yet another raucous time in Rio. A week after the race, they tested the new 308 and found it at least a second quicker than the pole position time for the Grand Prix. Great things were expected.

They came at the International Trophy race at Silverstone, a non-championship Formula One event that also included the top drivers from another series, F5000. Hunt had put the car on pole position by an astonishing 1.7 seconds from Peterson's Lotus and the 33,000 fans who turned up on race-day were ready to see the new British superstar win his first F1 race. They did, but in typical Hunt fashion, it was dramatic. He'd again been physically sick in the garage in full view of everyone before the race and then sat trembling and shaking in the car on the grid. His nerves were always there, but by now all his mechanics had become used to the odd behaviour and so were not concerned. One commented that it felt like the engine was shaking, despite it not being turned on!

Unfortunately as the race started, Hunt panicked and the gear knob came off in his hand with the clutch slipping leaving him fifteenth at the first corner. What followed was an incredible period of driving that saw him gradually ease back to the front before an audacious overtaking manoeuvre around the 160mph Woodcote corner, passing Peterson and taking the lead. He kept it to the end and as he crossed the line his team collapsed in tears of excitement and joy. Hunt's right hand was blistered and bloody after changing gear with the metal stub, but that was forgotten as he and the mechanics, plus Bubbles and Hesketh, sang a rendition of the Dambusters march to the adoring fans. Hunt had just won the fastest post-war race in Britain at an average speed of 133.58mph.

In the spring of 74 Hunt, on the advice of his business manager, moved to Spain to save on the crippling taxes that were being imposed in Britain at the time. He cancelled the lease on his London flat, 'acquired' the Porsche of his boss Lord Hesketh, and set off for the Costa del Sol. He was 'absolutely home-less' when he arrived and stayed in numerous hotel rooms whilst looking for somewhere to buy. It was a depressing experience for the fun-loving Hunt who very quickly realised that he was in a country where the weather was always hot, he couldn't speak the language, he had nowhere to live and was totally alone. The last two were dealt with in equal measure when he met Suzy Miller.

Brought up in Rhodesia, Miller was a stunningly beautiful blonde model who had also relocated to Spain and was alone. The two came together at the right time and within weeks they were living together in her flat. Sadly it wasn't the 'hearts and roses' romance that she in particular craved. Suzy wanted a long term commitment and certainly didn't want to be a casual girlfriend of a racing driver, a sport she knew nothing about at all, and soon Hunt was banished from her home. Using all of his charm he talked his way back into her arms, and then after numerous splits, he proposed marriage. It was the only way it seemed to make her happy, and so James half-heartedly asked her to marry him and a date was set for October 1974, immediately after the last race of the season.

It was clearly a mistake and as the date got closer, his cold feet became icy. Why he had suddenly exchanged his bachelor-lifestyle for a woman who he later admitted he didn't love despite her beauty, is a mystery. She was loving and affectionate and deeply loyal, the kind of partner most men would be enraptured by, but not James.

At his engagement party in London, he met his old girlfriend Ping and confided in her that he didn't want to go through with it, yet as the wedding had been paid for by Lord Hesketh (who would be best man) and would be held at Brompton Oratory in central London, he felt he couldn't let anyone down. A full symphony orchestra was booked and guests for the day included Graham Hill, Stirling Moss and Ronnie Peterson.

In the week preceding the big day, James went on 'four days of the most stupendous bender of his life', and even on the day he was drinking until 6am. A couple of Bloody Marys settled him, but the whole ceremony was conducted in an alcoholic haze and if Suzy Miller thought she had found the man she wanted to spend the rest of her life with, she would soon become disillusioned. The honeymoon was shared with Bubbles and his new bride in Antigua and for the entire time, both Hunt and his racing manager enjoyed themselves and hardly paid any attention to their new-despairing wives.

This all overshadowed what was a slightly underwhelming season in F1 for Hunt and Hesketh. After the victory at Silverstone, he struggled to establish himself at the front of the grid, although three third-place podium finishes in Sweden, where he had a lengthy scrap with Lauda's Ferrari, Austria and America meant he finished the season in eighth place in the Championship. It wasn't quite what the racing fraternity in the UK expected, especially as he was now seen as the natural successor to the now-retired Jackie Stewart, but in terms of his public persona, he was all-conquering.

His name was in all the gossip columns, regularly linked with numerous females despite his impending marriage, and as the team increased in size, so did their partying and extravagance. This was never more in evidence than at Monaco where the new boat, Nefertiti, was one of the largest in the harbour, plus the new helicopter and various expensive cars that were used just to chauffeur guests from one party to the next. The team partied wildly, helped by their pop star driver, but after Silverstone, they were now being taken a little more seriously by the paddock. What they needed now was to win a Grand Prix.

They needed to win to finally prove to everyone that they could take that further step, but it was also needed as finally the opulence and the extravagance was literally beginning to cost. Even for a man of Lord Hesketh's means, Formula One, then as now, was cripplingly expensive. The season had been disappointing and as a Grand Prix victory would mean around £14,000 to the team in prize money, it was essential that they start to win.

The austerity measures came into effect for 1975 where the car was only updated and not replaced, the helicopter was sold, the yacht didn't appear at Monte Carlo, and the mean machines were replaced by a Vauxhall Chevette. Even Lord Hesketh spent sometime selling T-shirts at Grands Prix in a way of raising cash. For James Hunt, now super-fit after spending most of his days in Spain running and playing tennis, much to the chagrin of his wife, the stringent policies meant he only received half his retainer, but decided to keep the Porsche as a consolation.

CHAPTER TEN

A win for Hunt, but a title for Lauda.

The contrast between the under-financed British team and the might of Ferrari could not have been starker. Whilst the one-driver outfit struggled to be competitive in a now underdeveloped and under financed car, the two pronged attack by the 'Prancing Horse' was fully unleashed as a World Championship was almost demanded. Lauda was clearly the number one driver, but Regazzoni was there as not just support but competition too. Ferrari were hot favourites to take the title from Emerson Fittipaldi, who was now looking for his third.

The opening round in Argentina actually saw Hunt shine with an incredible second place behind the Brazilian, his highest ever finish in a Grand Prix, but again he'd thrown away a victory after taking the lead on lap 26, only to spin off nine laps later and have to 'settle' for second. Again 'Bubbles' Horsley went public with his criticism and for the first time Hunt was under severe pressure at Hesketh. Lauda faired much worse with a sixth place finish, followed by a fifth in Brazil two weeks later just ahead of a far more conservative Hunt, clearly stung by the criticism he'd received.

In fact the early part of the season gave no clues as to how it would result. Both drivers, in their respective teams, struggled to gain results, although in the non-Championship International Trophy race at Silverstone, Hunt took pole and Lauda took the win. Neither mattered. It wasn't until the Spanish Grand Prix that Lauda's Ferrari started to look the part. In fact he and Regazzoni closed out the front row, but a crash at the first hairpin, caused by Vittorio Brambilla, eliminated them both. It was a huge accident, and the Montjuich Park circuit in Barcelona had nearly been boycotted due to safety concerns. The drivers turned up and midway through the race, Rolf Stommelen's Hill car lost its rear wing, flew over a guardrail and killed four spectators. Just another addition to the catalogue of disasters that the sport was recording.

Hunt had again briefly led that race before crashing, and at Monaco the low point of the season was reached when he crashed yet again. He spent the remainder of the race stood trackside shaking his fist at the McLaren of Jochen Mass, who he believed had pushed him off. This wasn't the first time he'd displayed this kind of behaviour, as the previous year he'd done the same with Emerson Fittipaldi, who at that time was on his way to a second World Championship. It was now clear to Lord Hesketh and Bubbles Horsley that something had to be done about their wayward driver and the 20 strong workforce of Hesketh Racing.

A meeting was called at Easton Neston where harsh words were exchanged and a plan to move forward was devised. It was felt that Hunt's living in Spain had caused a problem and so he agreed to visit the factory in between races so as to be better prepared for each race. His lifestyle was the subject of concern and he was told in no uncertain terms that he could not affect the success of the team by his drinking and partying. It seemed to work.

On the 22nd June 1975 James Hunt won his first Formula One Grand Prix and realised an ambition for both himself and the Hesketh team. Amongst the sand dunes of Zandvoort in Holland, Hunt put his car third on the grid and then in a wet and dry race, he timed his pit stop for new tyres to perfection. After intense pressure from Lauda for twenty laps, he crossed the finishing line just 1.06 second ahead of the snarling scarlet car. Afterwards the Austrian said he had settled for second in his quest for the title, but nothing could be taken away from Hunt that day. He had driven a superb race and the thousands of British fans who were dotted around the hills cheered manically. As Hesketh himself said: 'It was a wonderful feeling to know that those people, who had travelled with us all the way around Europe and had seen frustration after frustration, finally saw the result they wanted'.

Hunt partied that night like only he could, staying at the circuit and inviting fans to bring beer along in what became an all-night binge. His wife Suzy was missing. She had been to a few races but had become bored very quickly and had not been present at her husband's finest hour. In a way it was probably for the best as all of Hunt's party instincts were present that evening. Their marriage was unravelling, although publicly that was not acknowledged, and Hunt was trying to find a way out. He'd offered to buy her a flat in London and support her, but she refused and continued to share the marital home, if no longer the marital bed.

Hunt's first Grand Prix win in Holland

For Hesketh it was their greatest moment, although the rest of the season did still supply some good results. They finished second in France and Austria (the race that saw American Mark Donohue die in a practice accident, witnessed by Hunt) and ended up the season in fourth place in the Driver's Title race, a remarkable achievement by the small and now critically under financed team. In fact on the 14th November, the team announced it would close down as the £300,000 of sponsorship money that Lord Hesketh had reluctantly chased was not forthcoming. The next day at Thruxton, shown live on BBC's 'Grandstand' programme, James did a few demonstration laps in the Dutch-winning car before saying his goodbyes. Hesketh Racing was no more, although Bubbles did run a Hesketh for two more seasons with rent-a-car drivers, but with hardly any success. After his most successful Formula One season and his first victory, James Hunt was without a drive.

For Lauda, after the debacle of Spain, his season just rocketed. He took pole at Monaco and then won, giving Ferrari their first win in the principality since 1955. That was followed by victories in Belgium, Sweden, France and the US, plus numerous high placed finishes. His team mate Regazzoni won in Italy, but Lauda's record of nine pole positions and five victories in the season was proof that he was the best driver on the grid. He was described as an 'automaton' or had a 'computer-mind', and some critics felt he had no bravado in his driving style. No matter, the facts were that he accumulated 64.5 points and won the World Championship by nearly 20 points from Emerson Fittipaldi. The young and at times shy man from Vienna, who had built up a frightening debt to finance his dream, was now on top of the motor racing world. He had given the most famous team in F1 a title for the first time in over a decade and he had become the most famous sportsman in Austria (after becoming only the second man from that country to win an F1 title) and especially in Italy, where he was quite simply idolised.

His new found fame and fortune meant that his lifestyle changed dramatically. He put some thought into starting up his own small airline business, and was able to build a huge house in a village called Hof, near Salzburg. It has not been recorded what his family, and especially 'Old Man' Lauda had thought of his rise to success, but the days of falsehoods and subterfuge when trying to hide his racing ambition had clearly been worth it.

James Hunt and Niki Lauda approached 1976 with different mindsets. Hunt was out of a drive and wondering if his Dutch victory would be his career-pinnacle, whereas Lauda was World Champion and looking to defend it with an even stronger and faster car. Both had their off-circuit personal dramas to contend with and both were the most recognisable sportsmen in their field, but neither had any inkling that the next twelve months would change them both, independently and together, in the most dramatic and spectacular fashion.

First win for Ferrari at Monaco for 20 years and a title for Lauda!

CHAPTER ELEVEN

Head to head on and off the track

For as long as Formula One remains a sport, the 1976 season will surely always be regarded as one of the most exciting, dramatic and certainly defining in its long history. The twists and turns, political intrigue and soap-opera antics made it the greatest of all motor-sporting encounters that quite simply changed its face forever. It was the season that saw the peripheral sport suddenly burst onto the world stage with a force that meant it could never be ignored again. The money that had swilled around the paddock suddenly multiplied immeasurably after the final curtain was drawn, and the two main protagonists in the gladiator contest, Hunt and Lauda, became more famous, more respected and certainly more rewarded than ever before. Certainly Formula One in that season transformed itself from a sport that was just for the manically-interested to a global and world phenomenon.

Not that James Hunt had any inkling of any of that as 1975 rapidly drew to a close and he found himself seat-less. After the demise of Hesketh, he looked around for a top drive and was found wanting. Lotus spoke to him, but they wanted him to pay. It was never likely to happen, especially as on the day of the meeting they hadn't even bothered to buy him lunch. He spoke to Brabham about possibly driving a third car, but nothing came of it. It was looking desperate until he received a fortuitous phone call from the manager of Emerson Fittipaldi, World Champion in 1972 and 1974, telling him that the seat at McLaren would be available and he had better contact their manager Teddy Mayer pretty quickly. 'Emmo' had decided he was leaving McLaren and had taken the seemingly incomprehensible decision to join his brother Wilson's Copersucar team. There could be no other reason, apart from family loyalty, that lay behind Fittipaldi's decision other than the Brazilian sugar giant, who put their name to the car, were paying him a fortune to drive for the team. It was a decision that effectively ended his successful F1 career.

For Hunt there was no time to lose and within 36 hours he had signed as equal number one driver in the team alongside the German Jochen Mass. It was done with so much haste as pre-season testing was approaching, but it meant that Hunt would be paid a £45,000 retainer plus sponsorship funds from Marlboro, the main sponsor of the team. This of course came with its own obstacles as Hunt refused to wear any type of team uniform and certainly refused to dress in a presentable way for any type of function. The irony was lost on him that as he smoked 40 cigarettes a day, he was reluctant to wear the-then day-glow orange colours of the product he enjoyed so much. It was a match made in heaven on the track, but it was hell off it.

Teddy Mayer was the ruler of the McLaren empire, taking the team to most of its victories since the death of founder Bruce McLaren, and he had worked with many of the top drivers, but little could prepare him for the whirlwind that tore through the outfit in the shape of James Hunt. As Mayer would later say: 'What people choose to call talent these days, James had plenty of... but his outbursts led to some embarrassment from time to time, and it led to raised eyebrows as well'

Those raised eyebrows were visible at the opening Grand Prix of the season, in Brazil, when Hunt found the M23 (a car that had taken Fittipaldi to the Title two years previously) 'undriveable' due to the seat not being perfectly fitted to his frame due to lack of time since his signing, and in turn that meant the McLaren team was: 'a rudderless ship and didn't have any direction'. That was followed by a huge argument with Mayer about the set-up of the car during one of the many qualifying sessions that depicted a Grand Prix weekend in the 1970s, and against all advice he told the mechanics what settings the car should have and immediately went out and won pole position.

It gave him the gravitas very early on in his relationship with the team and from that moment on, he was the number one. There was little hope for Mass, who was mild-mannered in comparison, although many snarling despots throughout history could be compared the same way to Hunt, and it was clear that if McLaren were to win the title back, then it would be with the tempestuous but supremely-talented Englishman.

Calm before the storm, 1976 Brazilian Grand Prix

For Lauda, there were no such dramas as the season began. He was World Champion and feted wherever he went. The number one on his scarlet Ferrari looked like it belonged there and it was expected that it would stay there after the next sixteen Grands Prix too. If there were any clouds on the Lauda-horizon, it was the departure of his ally Luca di Montezemola to bigger things in the FIAT organisation. He was replaced by the young Daniele Audetto, a man who never at any time seemed to get along with Lauda and caused friction in their working relationship throughout their time together. No matter, Lauda went to Brazil, saw Hunt put his new car on pole and then promptly won the race himself.

Of course it wasn't quite as straightforward as that. Hunt had put the car on pole position, the first in his F1 career, but had made a poor start, running second behind Lauda until one of the engine's eight cylinders stopped firing. A fuel injector trumpet fell off, somehow trapping itself in the throttle so that Hunt spun into the catch-fencing and immediately retired. It was a disappointing start to his McLaren career, but many of the top men at Marlboro, who were less than impressed with his signing, seemed happy that he had made the ageing car competitive once more. It was also noted that Fittipaldi, in front of his adoring Brazilian fans, could only finish 13th in what was immediately obvious, a totally uncompetitive car.

Lauda took the win, the full nine points for victory and his customary position at the top of the Drivers' standings. After one race already, it was again the Ferrari and Niki Lauda who were the combination to beat.

It was at this time that the divide in James Hunt's marriage to Suzy was now beginning to show publicly. Privately they were estranged, but had kept up appearances, much to the dismay of poor Suzy, and over the Christmas and New Year period had visited friends in the skiing resort of Gstaad. Hunt no longer skied so as not to suffer injury, but had gone nonetheless as he wanted, he said, for Suzy to meet new people. That certainly happened.

After returning from Brazil, Suzy had called to say she was staying on in Gstaad as she was having such a wonderful time. James gave her his blessing and flew out to South Africa for round two of the World Championship. There of course he indulged in his own wonderful time dating the South African actress Paddy Norval followed very quickly by an exotic Portuguese lady called Carmen Jardin. It was manna for the tabloid press who now followed James all around the World as he was as sellable on the front page of the newspapers as he was on the back. The Playboy was always 'good copy' and the assignment given to any reporter and photographer to cover his every move must have been one of the most glamorous and certainly the easiest. Hunt led his love life publicly and didn't seem to care who knew about it.

Of course there was another ingredient thrown into the mix and that was of his wife. Her wonderful time in Gstaad had come because she had met the actor Richard Burton and the two had fallen in love, despite their 24 year age gap. Burton was one of the most famous actors in the world and his marriages to Elizabeth Taylor were of course the story of legend, but this hard-drinking, depressive yet brilliant Welshman fell completely for the young Suzy and later gave her credit for saving his life from the cocktail of drink and depression.

Soon Suzy was in New York watching Burton star in the new play 'Equus' on Broadway and as she was staying in the same hotel, it didn't take long for the newspapers to concoct the story that she was about to break the Burton-Taylor marriage. Hunt was tracked down in South Africa for his comments, and publicly he played the part of the disturbed and distraught husband saying: 'Naturally I am perturbed by the publicity surrounding my wife, but I must concentrate on the Grand Prix'. Privately he was pleased as Suzy had kept him informed and as far as he was concerned, she was now one less thing for him to worry about.

At the same time the news that Niki Lauda was about to marry Marlene Knaus became public, and although that too caused a stir in the Austrian and Italian press, it hardly registered on the scandal-richter-scale compared to James and Suzy.

In Kyalami, it was clear the 1976 season was going to be about these two. Hunt was again on pole with Lauda alongside and again in the race Niki took the victory, but this time James hung on to his tail and came in a creditable second. The reporters pursued James like no other and at this time his nickname had changed from 'Shunt' to quite simply 'Playboy'. In truth, he enjoyed it all, although he was forced to live in the house of a South African tennis player throughout his stay in the country to avoid the constant prying eyes of the press, but it was hiding a more serious issue. The World Championship was already two rounds old and Lauda had a one hundred per cent 18 points to just the six of Hunt.

The non-Championship 'Race of Champions' was next at Brands Hatch, won by Hunt with Lauda retiring with mechanical failure. It proved again that both were evenly matched on the circuit, but off it James was streets ahead. Niki was enjoying his honeymoon with Marlene, a fact all but ignored by the press, whilst James was canoodling with another model, Swedish bombshell Vanessa Hecklunk, in full view of the media and fans. The tabloids were overwhelmed and when they learned that James was about to fly to New York to 'confront' his wife, they went into overdrive. At Kennedy airport there were literally hundreds of reporters and photographers waiting to meet him and they all followed as he made his way to the hotel that Suzy was staying in. The fact that the two met for an hour and then James dropped Suzy off at Richard Burton's hotel immediately afterwards just added fuel to the flames. For his part, Hunt gave up giving quotes to the media about his marriage and prepared for the next Grand Prix in Long Beach, California.

CHAPTER TWELVE

Lauda takes control

The street circuit of Long Beach was devised by entrepreneur Chris Pook as an answer to the Monaco Grand Prix and it was hoped that some of the glamour of the principality could be created on the west coast of America. The truth was that the only thing the two venues shared was a proximity to the sea. Whereas Monaco was the haven of millionaires with their wealth displayed around the harbour in all its ostentatious glory, Long Beach could really only lay claim to the now permanently berthed 'Queen Mary' liner which had been transformed into a rather opulent but faded hotel. The streets on which the F1 cars were to race passed by run-down tattoo parlours, fast-food outlets and porn cinemas, only partially hidden by the convenient placing of fake palm trees. It was an ambitious project and in the early years a successful one, despite the Americans complete ignorance of most things Formula One. Although there was always a fan base in the States (mainly on the East Coast where the Watkins Glen race was run), most race enthusiasts in America were well served with Nascar and Indycar racing.

If the interest from the American media towards the first running of a F1 Grand Prix in Long Beach was underwhelming to say the least, then the antics of Hunt on and off the track and a hotel burning down during the race was to keep them amused if not entirely enraptured. Hunt, who had qualified third and never seemed at home on a street circuit, had an altercation with Frenchman Patrick Depailler's Tyrrell on the third lap and planted the car into the barrier. It was a typical racing accident where one driver felt the other hadn't given enough room, whilst the other felt he was right to attempt the overtaking manoeuvre, but neither of those personalities was James Hunt.

After climbing out of the car, he then spent some time stood at trackside shaking his fist furiously at Depailler each time he passed, much to the astonishment of drivers, fans and reporters alike. Two hours later, with Regazonni and Lauda filling the first two places in their Ferrari's and Depailler finishing third, Hunt's temper had not abated at all. Whilst the post-race press conference was taking place, with little being said of any interest by Lauda in particular, Hunt burst in and proceeded to verbally abuse Depailler, in the loudest possible terms. It was the bright spot of the weekend as far as the very bored American journalists were concerned as Hunt told the Frenchman that he should 'learn to drive' and that he had better 'watch out' in future. In fact from that moment Hunt never trusted Depailler again, right up until he was killed four years later in Germany.

The race had not done Hunt any favours at all apart from keep him in the headlines for all of the 'wrong' reasons again. It was felt that his McLaren car was sufficiently undamaged enough to have continued the race, but Hunt's mentality would not allow it. He had been cheated and that was the end of it as far as he was concerned. For Lauda, he must have watched with mild amusement as one of his main rivals for the title was having his own personal meltdown and he left America with 24 points to his name after just three races. Within a week he too was having his own inner crisis.

The Austrian, now newly-married and preparing a new life for himself and Marlene, had taken a few days off to work on his new house. Part of the work was to level off some ground as a new swimming pool was being built, but somehow Lauda – one of the fastest men on four wheels – managed to turn over his near two-tonne tractor and trap himself underneath, breaking two ribs in the process. He was in agony, but that paled into comparison once the Italian media got hold of the story. Some sections had always been unhappy that Ferrari never employed an Italian driver, and the fact that the current number one there was an Austrian, and a World Champion at that, made it more unpalatable. This was a gift to them and they proceeded to lambast Lauda publicly with every edition, so much so that the Austrian's response to one journalist was that he could not care less about what they thought or indeed what Ferrari felt too. It made him deeply unpopular with many fans and the cracks in the relationship with the Prancing Horse started to show at that early stage, despite the best efforts of a PR machine that went into overdrive immediately afterwards. Also his injuries were bad enough to suggest that he may have to miss the next race, but the amazing talents of Willy Dungl, described by Lauda as 'masseur, guru, dietician, layer-on-of-hands and the miracle-worker' ensured that his recovery was quicker than expected.

Whilst Lauda was recuperating, Hunt went to another non-Championship race, the 'Graham Hill International Trophy' at Silverstone, and won it in front of 75,000 ecstatic fans. The fact that Ferrari had refused to enter didn't take any gloss off the victory, and in truth it just helped to enhance the James Hunt image of playboy-cum-racer. On the track he was winning races and off it he was regularly dating gorgeous women, despite being married a lifestyle that suited the 70s. In fact the marriage came to an end shortly after the race, when after a final rendezvous in Spain with Suzy, she announced she wanted to marry Richard Burton, and their divorce was finalised in June. Two months later Suzy and Burton wed and she stayed with him for many years before the constant drinking took its toll and she left him. Burton then married Sally Hay who stayed with him until he died. Poor Suzy's choice of men seemed to be wanting to say the least. For James, he continued to do what he always did. He dated beautiful women, the British actress Joanna Petit among them.

In Spain, the fourth round of the Championship, Lauda raced with pain-killers to deal with his injuries, but he said he could feel his ribs grinding together each time he took a corner, so it was clearly quite uncomfortable. Hunt was now super-fit due to his extensive training regime, and it was his McLaren on pole with Lauda in second. Hunt's team-mate, Jochen Mass, was third so the cars looked like they were competitive and after a race long battle with the Ferrari, Hunt took the victory from a pained Lauda, whilst poor Mass had his engine expire with just a few laps to go. Again Hunt overplayed his emotions when he punched a man who had accidentally knocked a post race orange drink out of his hand accidentally. To be fair to James, he did feel guilty and tried to find the person afterwards to apologise, but was unsuccessful.

Everything seemed rosy in the McLaren garden with their first Championship victory of the season, but within hours that had all changed. The scrutineers had deemed that the car was illegal as it was too wide at the back wing by 1.8 centimetres! It was the ultimate irony that it should be a McLaren car that was disqualified as it had been theirs that had been the template for the new height and width regulations that had been introduced from the Spanish Grand Prix. It meant that the unsightly air-boxes behind the driver's cockpit had been replaced with more streamlined and flatter versions, and the existing models could all be modified with ease as opposed to redesigning completely early season. It also meant that the only car to be disqualified was Hunt's and so Lauda was promoted to the winner's position and his lead at the top of the standings increased with 33 points from 4 races, whilst Hunt had just six to his name.

The reaction from the McLaren team was understandably strong. Team Principal Teddy Mayer likened it to being given a death penalty for a parking violation, saying that there could in no way be any advantage for the car being 1.8 centimetres wider than the rest. Hunt of course lashed out, describing the team's failure to check such things as a 'fantastically sloppy performance'. The team left Spain, without James who returned to his Spanish villa, in turmoil. The upshot was that they radically redesigned the rear of the car by repositioning the oil coolers so as not to fall foul of the regulations again. It proved disastrous and very nearly cost them the World Championship.

In Belgium the car was frankly an embarrassment. Hunt somehow managed to qualify third, yet had been in so many near-accidents that drivers were questioning if he was now a danger on the track. The ill-handling M23 seemed to lurch dramatically at every corner and on a few occasions it was only his talent and bravery that kept it on the tarmac and not exploring the surrounding countryside. Patrick Depailler, who had been on the receiving end of Hunt's verbal assault in Long Beach described his driving as 'very wild', and so it was with relief to Hunt and indeed most of the drivers that the McLaren suffered a gearbox failure in the race and the lumbering orange-and-white car could no longer play the role of a mobile chicane as each driver tried to find a way past. Mass too suffered the same problem. Whilst Hunt and his team created their own crises, Lauda and Ferrari just strolled away with the win, finishing first and second with Regazzoni joining his team-mate on the podium.

The problems continued at Monaco where Hunt could only qualify down on the seventh row. The car was almost un-driveable and despite the removal of the airbox to help the aerodynamics around the rear wing, little seemed to make any difference. He ran only as high as twelfth in the race and at one stage lost so much interest in proceedings that he spun through a lack of concentration. That put him well and truly last and finally on the 24th lap, the

McLaren expired after an engine failure, seemingly out of sympathy for its driver's fate. Lauda of course won again and the lead of 45 points that he had over Hunt was so high that at no stage did anyone, not least Hunt himself, believe that the Englishman was in with a hope of challenging for the title. It seemed that the Austrian was comfortably easing to a second successive Formula One World Championship.

By the time the teams arrived at the Anderstorp track in Sweden, the McLaren mechanics were at the point of exasperation with the ill-handling McLaren. It seemed that nothing they could do made any difference and Hunt again struggled in qualifying, starting from eighth. For once the weekend wasn't dominated by Ferrari, but by the curious looking six-wheeled Tyrrells of Jody Scheckter and Patrick Depailler. They took pole, and after an entertaining dice with Mario Andretti's Lotus, they swept past the chequered flag in first and second with Scheckter giving the odd looking car its only Grand Prix victory. The Tyrrell was an unusual concept where the four small wheels at the front were supposed to minimise any aerodynamic drag, yet the large rear wheels surely negated that. This turned out to be their one and only Grand Prix victory and after persevering the following season, the idea was finally discarded and not seen again.

Lauda meanwhile had his worst race of the season, yet still finished on the podium, while at least Hunt completed the race, albeit down in a distant fifth place. He later said that out of the Grands Prix of 1976, Sweden was by far and a way his best drive. That confirmed how bad the McLaren M23 had become. Lauda's lead increased at the top of the standings and with the season approaching halfway, there seemed little chance of anyone challenging him. He had amassed 55 points and led the standings from Scheckter by 32 points. Hunt meanwhile had a mere eight to his name and the season was rapidly approaching halfway.

The two were good friends and respected each other highly on the track. James had this to say about his rival: 'He is very tough and finishes consistently. He is totally fair in overtaking and will always watch for you and if you get alongside he won't barge into you or make contact. He'll make himself as tough as he can in an absolute fair way. It means we can always have a clean race together'.

In France, both drivers were unwell. Lauda had a heavy bout of flu, whilst Hunt was feeling nauseous simply because he had overindulged in pate de foie leading up to the Grand Prix weekend. Thankfully for him, the upset surrounding his car was rectified as the McLaren mechanics decided to revert to the settings from the Spanish Grand Prix and suddenly it worked! From a lumbering tank of a vehicle, the M23 returned to its former guise of a winning Formula One car and Hunt set about putting it on pole position and winning with comfortable ease, despite the closing attentions of the 'not-to-be-trusted' Patrick Depailler. Lauda had a torrid afternoon, retiring on lap eight with a blown engine and a feverish brow. Suddenly and after exactly half of the season's races, there was a chink of light of hope in the long, black tunnel that Hunt had been trapped in. The gap to Lauda had been cut by nine points and he 'only' trailed by 38 with eight races to go.

If the 4th July 1976 had been a moment of celebration for James Hunt after the French Grand Prix victory, then the next day it was even more pronounced as an appeal against his Spanish Grand Prix disqualification was heard at the FIA headquarters in Paris, and with help of testimony from Lotus boss Colin Chapman, the decision was overturned and Hunt had been given the victory back. Not only had he been awarded an extra nine points, but Lauda lost three due to his demotion to second place. The appeal committee had rightly agreed that the extra couple of centimetres could not possibly have given Hunt's car an advantage. With the British Grand Prix next up, the Englishman's charge for the title was well and truly on. Suddenly there was a possibility of a British Formula One World Champion the first for three years, but Brands Hatch was again about to test the patience and the resilience of Hunt.

Hunt arrived at the British Grand Prix on the back of yet more media-bashing following a controversial Tour of Britain rally with the disc jockey Noel Edmonds. They had retired from the event after tyre problems and a collision with a tree and their disagreements afterwards as to whether they should continue or not, Hunt wanted to give up whilst Edmonds wanted to carry on, made front page headlines and again painted Hunt in a bad light. Edmonds said later that he was so embarrassed by Hunt's driving as they were being pursued by a police car that he actually leant out of the window and tried to cover up his name on the car with his arm as he didn't want anyone to know he was part of the rally.

Tour of Britain, enthusiastic Hunt and embarrassed Noel Edmonds

Hunt was one of the most famous British sporting personalities of the era and everything he did became news. It continued unabated in the lead up to Brands Hatch with a television appearance where he played the trumpet quite badly and that too was splashed over every newspaper.

Lauda meanwhile arrived in England on the back of contrived contract negotiations with Enzo Ferrari for the following season. Despite being the current World Champion, there was no guarantee that he would have a seat in the car in 1977, and after much discussion, where Lauda was allegedly called by the Old Man an 'insolent pig' and 'Jew-boy', they finally came to an agreement which would see Niki remain at Maranello for another year, and substantially richer in the process. It was just the way that Ferrari dealt with its drivers and Lauda wasn't the first, and certainly not the last, to be on the receiving end of such strange behaviour.

At Brands Hatch, a capacity crowd turned up to see Hunt qualify second alongside Lauda, but what followed in the opening corner of the race was to cause controversy not seen before. The McLaren again made a tardy start and lagged behind Lauda and his team-mate Regazzoni, but somehow the two Ferrari's managed to collide and the ensuing drama saw them, Hunt's McLaren and Jacques Laffite's Ligier all become entangled in a first corner carnage. The race was immediately stopped and Hunt somehow managed to get his damaged car back to the pits via a back road. He abandoned it and raced to get into the spare car as the grid lined up for a re-start. There then came an announcement from the PA system that only the cars that had completed the first lap would be allowed to re-start. This of course excluded James Hunt much to the anger of the 80,000 crowd. They vented their fury and the uproar that followed saw certain sections throw drinks cans at officials and on to the track. The din became intense, and fearing a serious disturbance, the stewards changed their decision and allowed all the cars, of which the main beneficiary was Hunt, back on to the grid to start the race. He had told them in no uncertain terms that he would be starting the race no matter what anyway and they would not stop him. They were clearly powerless and decided to let him race and make a decision afterwards.

The 'second' race, starting an hour later, was a far more orderly affair and Lauda again got away from Hunt and led him for 45 laps, but then to the delight of the now happy partisan crowd, the McLaren swept past the Ferrari approaching the Druids hairpin and was never headed after.

Hunt took the victory with his familiar two armed salute as he crossed the finishing line, with Lauda some distance behind. It was a perfect ending for every British motor-sport enthusiast, but as Hunt took the trophy and champagne, his victory was being protested by Tyrrell, Copersucar and of course Ferrari. The first two were gently persuaded by the stewards to withdraw their protests, but Ferrari announced they would take theirs to the FIA in Paris. For the moment though, Hunt had another nine points and was getting closer to Lauda with every race.

Winning the British Grand Prix then disqualification!

CHAPTER THIRTEEN

Lauda faces death

There will always be certain moments, dates and places in sport that effectively define the era. In Formula One that moment and that date was the 1st August 1976 and the place was the Nurburgring circuit in Germany. It is a fearsome place. Built in the 1920s and spanning 17 miles of undulating roads through forest-lined tracks with its twists and turns and climbs and swooping drops, it is impossible to marshal safely and any accident there could be unknown for an age as the remoteness prohibits help. Amazingly this circuit was still licensed for Formula One in the 1970s, although for the 1976 German Grand Prix the 'shorter' 14 mile track was used. In this age of health and safety and the demands that are made of modern-day Grand Prix circuits, it is astonishing to think that Formula One cars could lap one as terrifying as the Nurburgring at over 120 mph. Speaking before the race, Niki Lauda said that if he had an accident there it would be a 70/30 chance that he would die, whereas Hunt admitted that the place scared him. Most drivers were unsure as to whether they should race, but in a far more exhilarating age, they agreed that this was their job and they were being paid to be racing drivers.

Another problem with the circuit was the weather. It could be dry and warm on the start/finish line but wet and misty seven miles out on the other side. This was to be the case for the 1976 running of the race. Hunt had put his car on pole position despite his fear of the track, with Lauda alongside him and as the weather was damp, they and every driver bar one, Jochen Mass – decided to start on wet weather tyres. It soon became obvious that Mass, with his local knowledge, had made the right decision and after the first lap most came into the pits to change their tyres as Mass was simply charging through the field with his extra grip. Niki Lauda was one and he then re-entered the fray desperate to make up lost time. He was trailing badly with Mass leading his team-mate Hunt by 45 seconds when suddenly his Ferrari snapped right and hit the banking just before the right hand Bergwerk corner. It careered back into the path of Guy Edwards, Harold Ertl and Brett Lunger , bursting into flames and being hit by the latter two. All three drivers stopped and were quickly joined by Arturio Merzario and they all then attempted to extricate the Austrian from his burning wreckage. There were no marshals or safety amenities nearby, so they had to wade into the flames in their fireproof overalls. It took an age to get him out of the car and at one stage Ertl had to run to get a fire extinguisher to put out the flames that were engulfing Lauda. Eventually they succeeded, but the Austrian was badly burned and when the helicopter finally arrived, he was taken to hospital in nearby Koblenz. The race had been stopped, but few drivers were aware of the injuries that Lauda had received and most believed that he would be back in a couple of weeks in Austria.

Lauda's Ferrari after the near-fatal accident

The second race saw Hunt dominate completely and he won by over 30 seconds from Jody Scheckter with Jochen Mass in third. His first reaction on winning was to smile at the look on the McLaren manager's face. Teddy Mayer, or 'the Weiner' as James called him, had always wanted to win on this track and this was his first. His smile was from ear to ear and it also helped the team's World Championship bid as Hunt was now even closer to Lauda at the top of the standings. No one had any idea, except the four drivers who rescued him, of the extent of Niki Lauda's injuries and they all left Germany in reasonably high spirits and relieved to have departed unscathed.

Lauda's injuries were terrible. He had been flown to a specialist burns hospital in Mannheim where six doctors and 34 nurses tended him round the clock. He had first to third degree burns on his head and wrists, several more broken ribs and a broken collarbone and cheekbone. He had also inhaled poisonous fumes and toxic gases and the build-up of fluid in his lungs was life-threatening. There seemed little that anyone could do and on the Wednesday following the accident, a priest came in to give him the last rites. James Hunt said that he felt utterly hopeless and helpless when he heard the news and sent him a provocative telegram in the hope of igniting a fighting spirit in Lauda. It had become so very important to him that he should not die. Elsewhere, Chris Amon immediately retired from the sport and the Nurburgring was never to hold a Grand Prix in that form again. A German newspaper had taken a picture of Lauda whilst he was deep in a coma and headlined it 'My God, Where is his face?' The chances of the driver recovering were slim and suddenly the World Championship seemed inconsequential.

Following the accident, Lauda's team, Ferrari, announced that they would boycott the next Grand Prix in Austria as Enzo Ferrari, the 'Old Man of Maranello', believed that his team had been cheated out of victories in Spain and Britain. There was also a suggestion that the race in Austria would be cancelled in deference to their national hero who was fighting for his life, but this was never acted upon. As it was, Lauda was able to watch the Grand Prix from his hospital bed as his fighting spirit had brought about an astonishing recovery that had amazed even his doctors. His burns had been treated with the help of plastic surgery, although no attempt had been made to rebuild his right ear and his lungs were recovering from the scorching. He was still in a bad way, but no one could have believed that his recovery would be as quick as it had been.

How Lauda recovered is one of the great mysteries of the time. To all intents and purposes he was dead, yet his sheer will power and self-belief refused to allow him to slip away. Since that time, Niki has said that he has no memories of the accident at all, and no number of returns to the spot where it took place will trigger a response. He remembers travelling to the race, being stuck in a traffic jam and a fan pushing a photograph of Jochen Rindt's grave at him for no apparent reason. He remembers being told that a bridge had toppled into the River Danube that morning and thankfully the loss of life wasn't as great as it could have been, and he recalls leaving the pits after changing his tyres. Then nothing. The next recollection is of the helicopter as he is airlifted from the circuit. In his biography he admits that the accident has had no lasting psychological effect on him and the scars on his face – the mangled ear, the burns that stopped his hair from re-growing and the sight of skin grafted onto his eyebrows from other parts of his body – plays no part in his emotion. It is what it is. Only a supremely detached individual could surely cope with such a thing. Lauda was not only that but surely one of the bravest men ever to sit in a racing-car.

The race at the Osterreichring in Austria was poorly supported due to Lauda's and Ferrari's absence and it was a subdued grid that lined up to race on the sweeping circuit that lay on the foothill slopes in stunning countryside. Hunt had claimed pole position again and with the knowledge that his rival would survive and would almost certainly be back at a race track soon, it was a chance to gain more points in his absence. The start was delayed due to heavy thunderstorms and it was Hunt, who for once, made a great start from second placed man; John Watson in the Penske. He was soon taken and after damaging his car on a rock on the circuit, something that Hunt had no recollection of, he fell down the order and finished in fourth place for a valuable three more points. The race was won by Watson, who had promised to shave off his full beard should he ever win a Grand Prix after a bet with team owner Roger Penske. He was delighted with his win as was Lauda who must have allowed himself a wry smile when seeing that his Championship lead had only been reduced by three points in his absence. Not so happy were Hunt of course, and Jody Scheckter who had an enormous accident on the 14th lap, scattering debris all over the track and into the countryside. For the Penske team it was also an emotional victory, coming exactly a year after their driver Mark Donohue had died in the 1975 event.

The next Grand Prix was at Zandvoort, the Dutch and scene of Hunt's first victory twelve months earlier in the Hesketh. It took place on the 29th August and it just so happened to be Hunt's 29th birthday too. The omens were good again. Most of his family had travelled over to watch him in a race that he was now expected to win. He put his car second on the grid behind Ronnie Peterson's March, a driver who was showing the kind of late season form that suggested he was one of the quickest on the grid. Also John Watson was now a threat after his debut victory in Austria. A first win is like losing the burden on your shoulders for a racing driver and suddenly everything became easier and calmer when behind the wheel.

The race was an unusual one for Hunt as he found himself off the pace with an understeering car and in third behind both Peterson and Watson, who were having a private battle for the lead. This resulted in both making mistakes and Hunt gladly capitalised on the 12th lap and from then on he just maintained the gap whilst the March and Penske both eventually succumbed to mechanical problems. Hunt's only concern was the fast approaching Clay Regazzoni in the Ferrari. They had returned to Grand Prix racing after missing just one race, despite threatening to walk away completely and it seemed as if Regazzoni was there purely to stop Hunt from scoring points, but their tactic obviously failed.

As Hunt crossed the finishing line, he did his usual two arms in the air gesture only to lose control of the car and rapidly put one hand on the steering wheel whilst waving with the other. The birthday celebrations that night were raucous and long as there were now just two points separating Lauda and Hunt with four Grands Prix to go. Lauda had made his intention to be back behind the wheel soon very clear and so the race for the 1976 title was going to be as exciting as anything the sport had seen before.

CHAPTER FOURTEEN

The battle resumes

In between the Dutch and Italian Grands Prix, Hunt had flown over to Canada to take part in the 'celebrity' round of the Formula Atlantic series at Trois Rivieres, and although he struggled to finish third in a car alien to him, he did notice the talents of the man who won the race and eventually the series Gilles Villeneuve. So impressed with him, was Hunt, that he immediately arranged for Villeneuve to have a test drive in an F1 McLaren, and the following season the Canadian drove the third McLaren at the British Grand Prix at Silverstone which Hunt won and went on to become one of the most exciting Formula One talents of all time before his untimely death at the 1982 Belgian Grand Prix.

Meanwhile the media frenzy in Italy leading up to the Monza Grand Prix was taking on new levels. There were suggestions that McLaren and Penske were using illegal fuel (mainly due to their participation in the American single-seater series which used a far more explosive mixture which was banned in Formula One cars) and this was seized upon by the Italian journalists. Texaco, the fuel supplier, were aware of the allegations and made sure that their cars were exact in the fuel they were using, but the trucks carrying the petrol were held up at the Italian border by patriotic officials and so their arrival at the circuit was delayed. It was clearly a ruse to unnerve the British team as much as they could.

The big story of the weekend though was the amazing re-appearance of Niki Lauda. Just under six weeks after receiving the last rites from a Catholic Priest, he was in the Monza paddock preparing to race after missing just two races. He cut a stunning figure walking around the wet paddock, with his head swathed in bandages and people genuinely in awe of a man who had nearly burned to death in an F1 car, and now ready to race again. His return at the Italian Grand Prix meant that both he and James Hunt had finished exactly the same number of races that season, and now the real battle for the Championship could continue but the Italian officials had other ideas.

The weekend was wet and so Saturday's practice times, run in the dry, would almost certainly make up the grid, but it was decreed by the Italian stewards that in fact McLaren and Penske were indeed running on illegal fuel on the Saturday and so all three cars were put to the back of the grid. It was pure political farce as Texaco had checked everything stringently and in fact after the race the CSI and the FIA confirmed that in fact there was nothing wrong or in fact illegal about the fuel, but of course it was by then too late.

Hunt was forced to start from 27th place with Lauda unbelievably qualifying in fifth position. For the first time in history a French driver, driving a French car, Jacques Laffite in the Ligier started on pole position, but it was to be the March of Ronnie Peterson who won the race. Hunt had been enraged of course by his demotion and had charged through the pack and had managed to get up to twelfth on the 11th lap before tangling with Tom Pryce's Shadow and running off the circuit before bedding down in the sand trap. Hunt actually tried to get the car started again, but the race marshals would now allow it and he had the long walk back to the pits with the vociferous Italian fans booing and hissing his every step. Lauda though had driven an amazing race and finished fourth, just twenty seconds down on the winner. As he got out of his car, the bandages on his head were covered in blood, which proved what an heroic feat he had achieved. The title race was now back in his favour.

It was many years later that Niki admitted that he had in fact been scared when he returned to the paddock in Monza. He said that after the first practice session, he'd had to get out of the car as soon as possible, but publicly he'd put on a brave face. It changed the perception of him in Italy, especially with the ever-critical media, yet the feeling toward him from the team had also changed, but in a more negative way. The trust that had been shown before was now missing and Lauda didn't feel as if they were all behind him. The cracks that had started to show earlier were now widening, and they would increase by the end of the season. Add that to the fact that they had employed Argentinian Carlos Reutemann as a third driver in Italy, someone Lauda had a loathing for and it was clear that this marriage made-in-heaven was readily unravelling.

There were three races to go and before the Canadian Grand Prix at Mosport, Hunt flew to Toronto and competed in an International Race of Champions for European and American drivers. After that he looked for relaxation in his next favourite sport of squash. It was when he arrived at a club in the city that he received a message to call a Canadian journalist who told him the sickening news that Ferrari's appeal against Hunt's British Grand Prix victory had been upheld and he had been disqualified from his victory. The court in Paris had dismissed the evidence of Teddy Mayer and the video evidence from the RAC supplied by the BBC, whereas an appearance by Lauda, with a bloody bandage on his head, had clearly swayed their sympathy. It incensed Hunt and sadly his relationship with the Austrian started to detioriate as Lauda had been quoted as being delighted with the decision and felt it had been good for the sport. Hunt of course totally disagreed as it seemed to him that he had been cheated of a Grand Prix victory that he had won fair and square. It meant that the whole complexion of the Championship had changed and with just 27 points to be won, Hunt's task was now immense and seemingly hopeless. His reaction was understandable:

'Ever since I saw my first race as a kid winning the World Championship was all I wanted. I thought I'd got my hands on it and instead I'm screwed. You don't think I'm bitter?'

Hunt became depressed over the whole incident and his way of dealing with that was to drink and sleep with as many women as he could, something he was very successful at in Canada. A legendary tale of a private test session for McLaren ended with Hunt taking one of the female partners of the attending marshals aside and indulging his pleasures whilst the mechanics kept the unknowing man occupied with a tour of the car and the garage. Later a club singer fell for his charms and in between sets was taken away to his room, whilst at the same time James became drunker and drunker. The McLaren team, mindful of his state of mind, decided to let him relax in the only way he knew how.

It was at this stage that he and Niki had their first and only falling-out. The two teams were staying in the same hotel and when Ferrari manager Audetto attempted to convey his and their regret at the decision, he was told in no uncertain terms where to go. That was followed by Lauda telling the press that he was 'madly delighted' and with the possibility of a grudge match building between the two old friends, the journalists inevitably attempted to stoke the flames of the fire.

Hunt was so angered over the whole situation that he admitted that he attempted to 'inflame' it between himself and Lauda. The Mosport track for the Canadian Grand Prix was suffering from a lack of maintenance and as the two of them were leading the Championship, both were asked their opinions on racing there. Niki Lauda was understandably cautious, something which Hunt jumped on and said he was not interested in safety but in racing only. It was his way of 'psyching' out Lauda. The tension between the two of them was now intense and the press followed their every move.

Hunt had qualified on pole with Lauda sixth, but again had struggled at the start and allowed Peterson to get away. After eight laps though he passed and looked to be in control with a comfortable nine points in the bag. As it was though, the Tyrrell of Patrick Depailler started to close in second place, and after their collision at Long Beach earlier in the season, Hunt had a huge mistrust of the Frenchman and kept him in his mirrors at all times. The six-wheeled car closed uncomfortably on the McLaren and it was only with ten laps to go did the challenge fade away. It was later explained that a fuel line had ruptured in the car and had soaked Depailler's overalls and made him feel drunk! He said afterwards that he felt he'd driven ten laps with a bottle of Whiskey inside him….

Lauda finished eighth after a suspension problem, meaning that he'd failed to pick up any points and with his recovery still in its early days, it was remarkable that he was racing at all. It also meant that Hunt was back in the title race and thankfully for both of them, they met after the race and resumed their friendship. They both denied the quotes that had been attributed to them by the press and hoped that the final two races could be played out in a sporting manner.

One week later the Formula One 'circus' was at Watkins Glen in upstate New York for the penultimate race of the 1976 season. It's a sleepy area yet down the years has produced some of the most exhilarating races in history. The friendship between James Hunt and Niki Lauda had improved to such an extent that they had booked adjoining rooms at their hotel near the circuit. Hunt always rose at 8am no matter what, yet at seven on race day Lauda, knowing this, barged into his room wearing his racing overalls and announced loudly that 'today I win ze championship!!'. Hunt himself said he was no longer 'bothered' about the title as he still felt there was too much to do to make up the eight point deficit.

Hunt had the perfect weekend as far as results were concerned. Again he had put the McLaren on pole position, although he was pushed during practice by Depailler once more until an air bottle from his compressor fell off the car and hit the front two wheels of the Frenchman's car. That ended any hope of a Tyrrell pole. Lauda, now feeling stronger, put his Ferrari fifth and again well ahead of teammate Clay Regazzoni. Overnight it actually snowed, yet race day was warm and dry and the largest ever crowd at the circuit, 100,000– prepared for a possible Championship showdown.

Sadly it didn't turn out that way as again Hunt was left at the start by Jody Scheckter in the other Tyrrell. The two were great friends and so trusted each other on the track implicitly. Hunt actually described his driving after the race as like that of a 'grandmother', but he tracked Scheckter before passing him on the 36th lap, only to be held up by back-marker Warwick Brown four laps later and see the six-wheeled car overtake him again. For once Hunt contained his fury and went about re-passing Scheckter, which he finally did with twelve laps to go and so take his sixth official win of the season. Lauda had suffered understeer in a Ferrari that was becoming less and less competitive just when its driver demanded more and the World Champion brought it home in third place and four more valuable points.

After the race, James Hunt ignored the traditional champagne and decided to celebrate with a six-pack of cold American beer and then proceeded to enjoy the evening in a way only he could. The title race was now down to just three points with Japan as the season-ending finale and that evening was as raucous as anything seen before. Hunt had a realistic chance now of becoming the first British World Champion in three years, but also the first English World Champion since Graham Hill in 1968. Japan now awaited the drama.

For Lauda, the tension in the Ferrari camp was now tangible. Newcomer Carlos Reutemann was sent testing in France, whilst Lauda who was number one and of course still the current World Champion was effectively ignored.

The team didn't know what to make of the disfigured and seemingly disconnected Austrian, although publicly they kept backing him. Privately though, they seemed to have lost faith in his ability. It was no way to approach a Championship showdown and this probably led to Lauda losing his title.

CHAPTER FIFTEEN

Hunt for Glory

The final act of this sporting drama was to be played out in the unusual surroundings of the Mount Fuji circuit in Japan. The people of that country had little knowledge of Formula One, but did have a passion for the sport and so 80,000 fans crammed into the unique track curiously amused at the tension that accompanied the 'circus' as it came to town. The real fans, the ones who lived and breathed motor sport and knew exactly what was at stake, were back in Europe. For most of them, following Formula One in the 1970s was a frustrating affair as television rarely took an interest and radio reports were spasmodic. It usually entailed a wait for the following week when the specialised motoring magazines would publish a full race report. In the UK, only the British Grand Prix normally amounted to any television coverage, but such was the excitement building up to Japan that the BBC and ITV took the almost unprecedented step of televising the race live on the morning of the 24th October.

The Japanese believed that if you could see the peak of Mount Fuji, then you were in for a lucky day, so as the Sunday morning dawned and the mist gathered, it didn't bode well. Mario Andretti had put his Lotus on pole position with Hunt second and Lauda third, but race day looked like a non-starter from the beginning. It rained constantly and in the morning practice session many cars had slithered off the track without any grip at all. Marshals were then deployed to sweep the running water off the circuit as the organisers feared for their event and the hardy spectators huddled under umbrellas as the torrent continued. It seemed an unlikely ending to the most dramatic season in the history of Formula One, but the elements just served to add to its veneer.

For the main protagonists, Hunt and Lauda, they both approached the day in different moods. Lauda was understandably concerned at the conditions. It was after all just two months since he had been dragged from his burning Ferrari and nearly died, while Hunt had a far more light-hearted and liberal attitude. In fact at one stage, whilst the drivers, team owners and organisers discussed the merits of attempting to stage the race, Hunt actually walked to the pit wall in full view of the spectators opposite and 'had a tinkle' as he described it. He was cheered and hand clapped by the bemused but appreciative audience.

As the rain fell, at times in torrents, many drivers expressed a wish for the race to be cancelled or at least postponed until the next day, but there were television companies who had paid a lot of money to air the race and the organisers had invested around £1 million, a huge amount in 1976, to stage the Grand Prix, so it was finally decided that it would be delayed, but the Japanese Grand Prix would go ahead that afternoon.

When it finally did get underway it was Hunt who made a storming start from Andretti and immediately pulled out a lead, happy in the knowledge that he would not be driving into a blinding spray from any car in front of him. All he had to do was to stay there and the World Championship should be his even if Lauda came second, as he had won more races than him. By lap two that task seemed to be even easier as the Austrian slowly pulled his Ferrari into the pits and retired. For the first time in his life he had given up. The blinding spray made it almost impossible to see and his eyelids were still suffering from burns making it difficult for him to blink. The Ferrari mechanics fell on to the car expecting a mechanical problem, but Lauda just got out and had a quiet word with the team manager. For him his life was now more important than any World Title, and although the Ferrari team offered to give a mechanical explanation for his retirement, he refused. It was the manner of the man and he was admired by all for it. It is also worth mentioning that in fact three other drivers Larry Perkins, Carlos Pace and Emerson Fittipaldi all retired for safety reasons.

Sadly Enzo Ferrari's behaviour later that day toward his driver left a lot to be desired. At no time during the telephone conversation between the two did he ever ask about Lauda's welfare and seemed to be more interested in why he had retired, when in fact just fifteen minutes later the rain had stopped and the title could still have been won. The 'Old Man' was a maelstrom of emotions and opinions, but it has been said on too many occasions that his love of his drivers was not remotely close to his love of his cars.

Lauda withdraws from the 1976 Japanese Grand Prix

Back in the race, it must have been a huge psychological boost for Hunt when he saw the McLaren pit board sign saying 'NIKI OUT' but he admitted after the race that he felt sorry for his rival and friend and could understand why he had made the decision to quit. All he had to do now was to keep the car on the track and make sure he finished fourth or higher. There was a moment of concern though when he was attacked by the March of Vittorio Brambilla, a driver with an aggressive but fair temperament on the track, but he overshot a corner and spun. The concern was then replaced by relief as he saw his team mate Jochen Mass in his mirrors and for a while the German could play the role of 'rear gunner' to stop any more challenges, but in the terrible conditions, he lost control and retired with his front right tyre hanging from its bodywork.

Soon the worries that Hunt had came to realisation when he saw that the weather was finally easing and the top of the volcano could now clearly be seen. The track was drying and in his enthusiasm for winning, Hunt had not taken care of his tyres, which were now falling apart (like all drivers he had started on wet weather tyres) and they were now badly overheating. Soon he found himself hauled in by Depailler in the Tyrrell and then quickly by Andretti in the Lotus, dropping him to third and his title now in the balance once more. At this point Hunt needed the guidance of his team on the pit wall, but in an age before radio communications, all they could do was to offer a pit board that showed an arrow, which was an instruction to the driver that the mechanics were waiting with fresh, dry weather tyres. For some reason Hunt ignored it and continued to ignore whilst other drivers pitted, believing that a pit stop would ruin his race, but on the 68th lap it was taken out of his hands as a front tyre disintegrated just before the pits entrance. He quickly raced in and the McLaren mechanics changed all four tyres in just over 27 seconds, an age in today's era, but very quick for the 1970s. It as even more impressive as the car was almost completely flat on the ground due to the deflating tyres and the mechanics had to physically lift it to change the wheels as the jack couldn't fit underneath.

Hunt charged out back onto the track in a furious mood. He was down in fifth and his pit board seemed to be giving conflicting signals. Firstly they said he was fifth, then it said fourth and now third! He had no idea what was happening, but in his fury Hunt had driven like a demon and had passed cars at will, lapping back markers and also the third and fourth placed cars of Regazzoni and Alan Jones. Those final five laps had decided the World Championship, but as the chequered flag was waved for Mario Andretti's first Formula One Grand Prix victory, James Hunt was convinced he had been cheated of a World Title due to his team's bungling. As the day-glo orange McLarenM23 raced down the pit lane, the driver's mood matched the surroundings. The sacred volcano that towered over the area had been clouded in mist for most of the day 26th October 1976 before unleashing a torrent of rain that had almost destroyed the intentions of everyone present and so adding an almost surreal twist to the climax of one of the most thrilling Formula One World Championships in history. It was only when he climbed out the car to be greeted by the three fingers salute by all and sundry, that his desire to 'strangle' team boss Teddy Mayer evaporated.

Hunt is World Champion!

Even after the race had finished and Hunt had been on the podium, there was still a part of him refusing to believe that he was the Formula One World Champion. It was only when he returned to the pits and saw that everyone had packed up and gone home and he was also able to check the lap charts personally, that he finally allowed himself to accept it. There was no one to protest and no one to take it away. James Hunt was the 1976 World Champion.

The celebrations afterwards were suitably raucous in the dining room of the Mount Fuji circuit. It normally closed early, but Hunt and his entourage filled it and imbibed lots of Japanese beer. He had never liked champagne, which was a shame bearing in mind how much was on offer that season, and when he flew back to Heathrow the next day, it was with a huge hangover

Lauda meanwhile had flown back to Maranello to have a face-to-face conversation with Enzo. To his shock and amazement, Ferrari told him that he would be made sporting director for the following season, meaning effectively that his driving career with the scarlet cars was over. Only after Niki had retrieved his contract, signed earlier in the year, and threatened to join McLaren, did the Old Man defer, but told Lauda that Regazzoni had been fired and now Reutemann was the number one driver. It was a shocking way to treat a man who had nearly burned to death in one of his cars and as Niki said later: 'I had pretty much had my fill of Ferrari by that time'. It was hardly surprising, and the Austrian went away back to his home to spend time with his wife and prepare himself both mentally and physically for a new season.

The 1976 season really was a classic and in the best soap opera style it pitted two totally different characters against each other. Lauda had always been the automaton in a racing car. He drove to win and outside of the environs of the cockpit, he was a no-nonsense talker who did not suffer fools at all. Hunt was the opposite. He was the archetypal racing driver with a glamorous life and a playboy attitude to his set career. The fact that his wife, Suzy, had left him during the 1976 season for the actor Richard Burton, just added to his profile. Although it wasn't the painful break up that it was portrayed by the media, it gave him the chance to play on the sympathy vote. The two personalities were as different as chalk and cheese.

The season itself is also worth remembering for the fact it was the first one that did not see a death during a Grand Prix weekend, although Lauda's accident certainly came close to continuing that sad statistic. It's fair to say the battle between the two ignited an interest in the sport that hadn't been seen before and within two years multi-million pound sponsorship deals and the advent of television started to change it completely. Today it is almost unrecognisable from the image it portrayed back in 1976.

CHAPTER SIXTEEN

Party

One year previously when Niki Lauda had become World Champion, the celebrations were sombre and slightly muted. It wasn't in his character to do anything else. He had realised an ambition and now it was a case of preparing for the next one. Not so James Hunt.

The flight back to Heathrow was as raucous as possible with the in-flight alcohol running out very quickly and it was a very drunk and dishevelled Hunt who was greeted by 2,000 well wishers when he stumbled off the plane, including his family.

'I hadn't expected my family to be there and it was the most unnerving thing to have to say hello to them in front of all those people. It was all quite overwhelming'.

For the following few months his life was no longer his own with sponsorship events to attend, television appearances and regular celebrity bashes, all of which he loved and loathed at the same time. His personal attire continued to baffle, turning up in jeans and T-shirt for awards ceremonies and nearly always accompanied by his beloved alsatian dog Oscar. Thankfully he did dress for the occasion on the 17th December when he officially received his Formula One World Crown in Paris. He'd attended the Earls Court motor show where he was besieged, had personal appearances all over Europe and a special 'James Hunt' day at Brands Hatch, graciously attended by Niki Lauda, where 12,000 fans all wanted a piece of him. Sadly it was another example of James at his worst as he'd had a verbal disagreement with the circuit owners and management and the day was soured by his behaviour over extra tickets causing crowding problems in the clubhouse. It seemed he just couldn't help himself at times.

At a special BRDC evening, he became in his own words 'legless' and managed to get involved in a scuffle with a fellow guest after knocking his glasses off and somehow standing on them. It was pure theatre for him, but it wasn't something that he always enjoyed.

'My personal freedom is something I had worked at for so long and now it seems completely gone. I am simply not my own man anymore'. He was though still an attractive proposition to young and willing ladies with beautiful French model Valentine Monnier now on his arm at most functions, and predictably his dress sense failed to improve, turning up in a tatty T-shirt and ragged jeans with sandals when at least a suit and tie were expected. One man who found that almost too much to take was the three times World Champion Jackie Stewart, a man who always dressed immaculately for the occasion. As he pointed out, James dress demeanour hardly represented a man who was at the peak of his profession. It was something most people agreed with.

Sadly the adoration and fawning started to affect him and within months, Hunt's behaviour off the track started to affect his popularity. It was ironic as he said at the time that he didn't want his ego to be 'over-fed' and that he was anxious not to let it all get to him.

'I don't want to abuse people. I don't want to start believing all the flattery. It can lead to bad behaviour and I could end up being a very objectionable person'.

Whilst Niki Lauda was quietly preparing for the 1977 season, privately fuming over his treatment by the Ferrari team, James Hunt was anything but quiet and private and it would take them down separate paths from now on.

CHAPTER SEVENTEEN

Lauda rises and Hunt falls

As well as the World Championship crown, James Hunt won many other awards in 1976, some he would be proud of, but one most people would prefer not to recognise. It was that of the Prix Citron, the Lemon Prize for the most uncooperative driver of the year, handed out by the International Racing Press Association. In 1977 he won one of those awards again, and it wasn't the World Title. In fact he won the Prix Citron easily as his behaviour off the track plummeted to new depths. Experienced journalists, those who had travelled the world and dealt with drivers for decades, almost unanimously harboured a disliking for James Hunt. The dislike was especially prevalent in the British journalists, who in the past had dealt with previous World Champions like Jim Clark, John Surtees. Graham Hill and Jackie Stewart all representing their country with dignity and respect, something which could not be said for the loutish and boorish James Hunt. It became so pronounced that certain specialist magazines hardly ever carried interviews with him due to his behaviour, something which both the team, McLaren, and their sposnors Marlboro were unhappy about. Hunt had surrounded himself with 'hangers-on' who hung on his every word and laughed at his every joke. Any self-respecting scribe who entered the inner sanctum of the McLaren garage to talk to him, usually left after a ritual humiliation and ridicule. It is fair to say that James Hunt did not carry the weight of a World Champion easily.

Then again Niki Lauda was hardly the type of persona to engender a positive feeling as his detachment from those around him gave the impression of a coldness and aloofness that was probably more pronounced due to the man's desire to win another title. His emotional connection to the sport and his success could be seen perfectly in the fact that all the trophies he won in his career were given to a garage proprietor near his home in Austria. He seemed to have little time for his fans, but at least he attempted to treat the press with respect. He wasn't sought out as much though as most of his answers to questions were one-dimensional and frankly rather dull. There was the paradox.

Hunt was entertaining and always provided great 'copy', but he was unpleasant and unwelcoming, whereas Lauda was respectful, but boring.

Before the season began, a test session was scheduled at the Paul Ricard circuit in France. The night before Hunt had joined Lauda at his home in Salzburg where according to Niki: 'We had a helluva time, drank and smoked far too much, but he outlasted me and I went to bed earlier than him'. Lauda was due to fly them to the South of France in the morning, and when Hunt hadn't turned up at the airfield on time, he was ready to go until he saw James and an Austrian lady fall out of a taxi in a dishevelled state on the runway and board the plane both the worse for wear. They both slept soundly throughout the flight. Later, during the test session, James had felt so tired that he simply parked his McLaren by the side of the track and fell asleep until manager Teddy Mayer fearing the worst ran to the car and woke him up. He was promptly sent to his hotel to sleep it off.

For the opening race of the season, in Argentina, the organisers had asked for the World Champion to attend a function to promote the Grand Prix. They were shocked and outraged when Hunt turned up in an unkempt state, wearing a scruffy T-shirt and dirty jeans. It was clear that being the Formula One World Champion was not going to change him. Sadly it wasn't going to guarantee results either and a broken suspension helped the car to plough into the barriers on the 32nd lap, an ignominious end bearing in mind he'd taken pole again. Lauda had retired with mechanical problems, whilst the new team of Wolf-Racing won on its debut with Jody Scheckter.

By the time the 'circus' had arrived in Brazil two weeks later, Hunt had been arrested for driving a hire car with no licence. The police had actually been quite relaxed about the whole affair, getting him to pose for autographs whilst the missing document (which had been stolen the previous year) was overlooked, but the Brazilian press made a huge story out of it and he again was front page news for the wrong reasons.

Not that he helped his cause too many times. Before the Grand Prix, Hunt had suffered terrible food poisoning and then had played a marathon twenty hour game of backgammon in the hotel which only finished hours before opening practice. Hunt's session on the track was interrupted constantly by pit stops as he rushed to find the nearest toilet as the poison lingered in his body. Despite that, he still won pole position once more and managed to finish second to Lauda's team-mate Reutemann whilst the Austrian could only secure a third place.

There was a brief break before the next race in South Africa, and whilst Niki Lauda got on with the important business of testing the car that had so far only yielded four points for him, Hunt again disgraced himself in front of dignitaries at an important function. This one was a gala held at the Europa Hotel in London where the best of the British motor racing fraternity were to be honoured, in the presence of HRH the Duke of Kent. Hunt was awarded the Tarmac Trophy with prize money of around £2,500 and made an amusing and gracious speech, yet his attire of T-shirt and jeans again led to comments of disapproval from most there. Again he made the newspapers and this time it was with a sense of irritation as opposed to amusement that greeted the headlines. To turn up at a gala function, hosted by Royalty, and effectively in his honour and to dress the way he did was now being described as 'childish' and of course 'totally disrespectful'. The relationship between the headline writers and Hunt was as strong as ever, but only one side was now benefitting from it.

John Watson a respected and successful Formula One driver and who raced against Hunt many times had this to say: 'Perhaps I am more conformist, but if you are going to a function which is held in your honour, you dress accordingly. He seemed to take pleasure in wearing jeans, like he was taking the mickey out of everyone. I think it's wrong to deliberately antagonize or confront people, whose standards are not necessarily yours'

Lauda had his own problems in the shape of his team-mate Carlos Reutemann. After two races he had won in Brazil and acquired 13 points to Lauda's four and was now clearly seen by Ferrari as the number one driver. Lauda had always disliked him and had campaigned vigorously to keep his previous partner Clay Regazzoni, but with no success. It was clear what the powers-that-be at Ferrari were doing. They had lost faith in Lauda after his Nurburgring crash and seemed to be attempting to demean him, despite him winning the title in 1975. Lauda was made of sterner stuff though, as his recovery from the accident had proved, and he determined that he would regain his number one spot within the team. To that end he persuaded Mauro Forghieri to schedule a private test session to iron out the aerodynamic deficiencies that the new car seemed to have. It worked perfectly, especially as Reutemann was not involved and the team could approach the South African Grand Prix with confidence. Sadly the race would be remembered for more Hunt-grabbing headlines and another fatal accident that completely overshadowed a Ferrari revival that sowed the seeds for a Lauda title charge once more. Again Formula One racing in the 70s showed how dangerous and fragile it could be.

CHAPTER EIGHTEEN

Lauda charges ahead

James Hunt very nearly wasn't allowed into South Africa after a particularly raucous flight from the UK. He had found himself in First Class, something he very rarely bothered with to save money, and had drank most of the alcohol available, and in a usual state of inebriation had attempted to persuade fellow passenger, pop star Leapy Lee to sing his famous hit '*Tie a Yellow Ribbon*' to a daughter of the famous De Beers family. As this failed, James then spent most of the flight serenading the passengers himself, much to their chagrin and annoyance. Complaints were made and customs took a dim view of the proceedings. He was eventually allowed into the country to compete in the Grand Prix.

The race saw Hunt take pole and Lauda win with ease, his first victory since his horrific crash, and in a way it soothed the demons that were playing in his mind and it also proved to the doubters, of which there were many, that in fact he still had the mental and physical ability to win races. Sadly the Grand Prix will be remembered for another horrific fatal accident that claimed the life of one of the sport's potential stars.

Tom Pryce a Welshman was in the Shadow when he came across two marshals running across the track to attend to a minor accident involving his team mate Renzo Zorzi. There was a small fire, but it was of no real consequence, and so the marshals with hindsight had no need to take the actions they did. The first made it safely, but the second burdened by a heavy fire extinguisher had no chance and Pryce's car ploughed into him, killing the driver instantly as the extinguisher hit him face on. The car didn't slow and hit the crash barrier at 160mph, colliding with Jacques Laffite's Ligier. It was another terrible accident and marred Lauda's victory, whose car had been affected after a piece of the Shadow's roll-bar had jammed itself under the Ferrari. Hunt was understandably scathing of the safety measures, or lack of them, in the Formula One racing.

'I have been saying ever since I became a Grand Prix driver that until there are professional marshals trained to a high standard and with suitable experience there will be unnecessary deaths or injuries in motor racing'

It was true that the sport still seemed at times to have a death wish and many drivers would just take the line of 'there but for the grace of God go I'. Too many drivers were killed in pursuit of their sport and it took too many years for the problems to be adequately addressed.

Lauda enjoyed his victory, although his ribs had started to cause problems a result of his crash in Germany and it hardly helped when Enzo Ferrari publicly questioned his fitness in the Italian press. By this time Niki was looking for a way out of the team and there were overtures from Bernie Ecclestone's Brabham team for the following season, but it would take a few months before any deal could be discussed. Whatever would be agreed, it was sure that he would be financially rewarded. Not so Hunt. He had officially become the cheapest World Champion taking into account inflation - earning in the region of just £160,000 for 1976, although that would increase the following season to around £600,000 from sponsorship and corporate marketing, but in terms of his playboy profile, there was no one who could come close. After dating more beautiful women, he fell into a relationship with Jane 'Hottie' Birbeck, the daughter of a Brigadier and who was to get as close to him as any other woman would, but almost by accident.

They had a long-distance relationship as she worked for a photographer in New York, meaning that the two could only get together sporadically. It put a strain on the relationship and at one stage they parted, only for Jane to realise she was pregnant! That meant James flying to America to pick her up and set her up in his home in Spain. Sadly she miscarried and that was followed by others too, but it seemed as if at long last Hunt had found a partner he wanted to be with for more than an evening.

On the track, Lauda was charging towards his second World Title. He recorded second places at Long Beach, Monaco and Belgium, sandwiching a non-start in Spain due to yet more excruciating pains from his ribs, but his success was hardly endearing him to either the fans or the motorsport press. They again accused him of driving like a robot and one headline stated that he only 'did what was necessary and has no flair'. It mattered not to the Austrian as he took a commanding lead from his closest rivals, Mario Andretti in the Lotus and of course Hunt. At Zolder in Belgium, Niki earned his nickname 'The Rat'. It came about after David Purley, driving the LEC car, held him up for a few laps too many whilst nursing rapidly deteriorating tyres and after the race Lauda had confronted the Briton in the pits. Purley, a man not to be messed with either on or off the track, was singularly unimpressed and described him as a 'rat', referring to his facial appearance. Hardly pleasant but it was a moniker that stuck for the rest of his racing days.

The World Champion unimpressive at Long Beach in 1977

Whilst Lauda was racking up the points, Hunt earned one with a sixth place finish in Spain. What was more concerning to the Englishman was a 'kiss and tell' story by a Dutch journalist, Alissa Morien, who had come to interview him about his career, but the two ended up in bed and their exploits were then splashed all over the magazine shortly afterwards. It was clear she had set him up, and if Hunt took this kind of thing in his stride, then it wasn't known how Jane Birbeck viewed the whole sordid affair. By the same token, it was inconceivable that James had no idea what was happening, bearing in mind his vast experience of the opposite sex.

In a case of symmetry, James Hunt won the British Grand Prix at Silverstone after inheriting the lead from the perennially unlucky John Watson with a quarter of the race to go. 'Wattie' had lost the previous Grand Prix in France on the last lap after running out of fuel and Niki Lauda won the German Grand Prix, where he was still highly regarded and came second in his home race in Austria. The two also spent some time at Hunt's villa in Spain where predictably a good time was had and after enduring an airline strike, Hunt then turned up five hours late, dressed scruffily, for the launch of a book that catalogued his Championship-winning season. His appearance in the trade-mark T-shirt and tattered jeans didn't impress everyone.

CHAPTER NINETEEN

The pendulum swings again

James Hunt relinquished his crown meekly as he failed to score any points in most of the second half of the season due to a combination of mechanical problems and driver errors. He did hang on to the Prix Citron trophy with some ease though, as his fractious relationship with the press plummeted to new depths as most journalists preferred just not to interview him rather than endure yet more childish antics from his entourage. It had been noted by the McLaren team that his name hardly ever merited a mention in the specialist press outside of race reports and his sponsors must have felt nothing but exasperation at the situation. One esteemed journalist actually wrote him a letter complaining about his behaviour, and surprisingly received a response from Hunt apologising and feigning ignorance. It didn't make much difference as Hunt's cronies continued to play up to him at every opportunity.

Lauda was nearly Champion for a second time by the time he arrived in Holland for the race at Zandvoort, but so tired was he of the politics and lack of support at Ferrari, that he finally signed the deal that would take him to Brabham for the following season. It was kept a secret from everyone, including both teams' personel in Holland, a race remembered for a coming-together of Hunt and Andretti around the notorious Tarzan hairpin. This resulted in a huge argument between the two and Hunt shouting at Lotus boss Colin Chapman that his driver would never win the title until he stopped hitting people on the track. Andretti thereon went on to win the 78 Championship with some ease. The two did 'kiss and make up' afterwards and had a healthy respect for each other from that moment onwards.

In Italy Lauda virtually became World Champion for a second time, but it was greeted in a muted fashion by all involved with Ferrari as news of his departure became public. Enzo spoke to the press and described Lauda as 'that Judas who sold himself to the rivals (Alfa Romeo who supplied engines to Brabham) for thirty kilos of salami'. The press turned on 'the Austrian' as he was now described and in this heated atmosphere he finished second and then travelled to Watkins Glen where he finished fourth, a race won by Hunt in supreme fashion, and took the title for the second time.

Whatever joy he had personally at becoming World Champion was demeaned publicly by the Ferrari team and seemingly most of Italy. He had been described as a 'trembling coward' by the press after withdrawing from the Japanese Grand Prix the previous season and after a huge row with the team in Canada, where they then sacked his personal engineer Ermano Cuoghi, who had rather foolishly announced that he too was off to Brabham, Lauda simply walked out and refused to race at Mosport Park or Japan. This was greeted with anger by the fans, the press, the race organisers and of course the sponsors, but Niki had frankly had enough. He had secured his second World title and in his time at Ferrari had won 15 times, secured 23 pole positions and given them the World Championship twice. One man who backed Lauda's decision to go back to his home in Austria was Hunt who empathised with his decision and said he would do the same in his position.

Hunt himself left his best driving of the year to those final three races where after the victory in America, he led the Canadian Grand Prix only to crash into team-mate Jochen Mass as he was lapping him. After spending a few laps at the side of the track shaking his fist at the bewildered German he then promptly flattened a marshal who was trying to stop him from running across the track. He was fined 2,750 Canadian dollars for the incident and again he was splashed all over the front pages with headlines such as 'Hunt the Punch'. He was now the object of amusement in the United Kingdom, where non-race enthusiasts had tired of his exploits, whereas the real fanatics were just hopeful of another glimpse of the talent that had taken him to the title twelve months previously. That glimpse ironically was from the other side of the Atlantic ocean and few British fans actually witnessed it.

At the final race, again missing the World Champion who was sat at home watching from the comfort of his living room, Hunt won easily, but the race was overshadowed by an incident that saw Gilles Villeneuve's Ferrari collide with Ronnie Peterson's Tyrrell and fly into the spectators killing two instantly. The mood darkened after the race when both second placed man Carlos Reutemann and Hunt left quickly to catch a plane from Tokyo airport, leaving just Patrick Depailler to stand on the podium alone. The organisers, already running a race that didn't include the current World Champion, were less than impressed and threatened to fine the drivers. Nothing came of it and the 1977 season ended with Niki Lauda winning three races and becoming World Champion again and James Hunt also winning three races but holding on to his title as the most 'un-cooperative driver of the year' award.

CHAPTER TWENTY

A new era

The new World Champion started the new year with a new team. After the political wrangling and in-fighting of Ferrari, joining the British team of Brabham founded by Australian Jack Brabham but now run by Bernie Ecclestone was a clear breath of fresh air after a suffocating confinement that had actually brought success to both parties. Sadly the relationship with the Chessington-based team never matched the potential that had been expected and Lauda found 1978 a frustration. The problem lay in the fact that Ecclestone now had bigger ambitions outside of just running his own Formula One team. He wanted to run the sport of Formula One, and was now on his way to achieving that aim and so effectively left the management of Brabham to his brilliant engineer Gordon Murray. A second problem was that Brabham were in a deal to use the unwieldy Alfa-Romeo engines, which immediately affected any competiveness the car may have had, and that was added to the fact that Colin Chapman had again produced something quite special for his Lotus team.

Chapman was a flawed genius. He would time and again design a car of such breathtaking advancement that the rest were quite literally left in their wake taking the likes of Jim Clark and Emerson Fittipaldi to World Championships. The main criticism, mainly from the drivers who had to race the cars, was that they were liable to break at any time and so become shockingly dangerous. Despite that, Lotus were one of the most successful teams in motor sport, and for 1978 a car of such jaw-dropping beauty was designed for ostensibly Mario Andretti and his number two Ronnie Peterson to contest and win the Championship. It was the Lotus 79, a natural successor to the first 'ground effect' car that had made its debut the previous season, the 78. Ground effect was a new phenomenon in the sport where aerodynamics and spoilers (ie wings effectively turned upside down) created a suction that simply glued the car to the floor and so made it feel as if it was driving on rails. The speeds this created had never been experienced before and the g-forces encountered by drivers at cornering speeds tested their fitness and their bravery. The Lotus 78 had been moderately successful in 1977, yet no team or engineer had taken notice and attempted to replicate the design, and so in 1978 the Lotus team quite simply swept all before them with Mario Andretti almost strolling to the Title. The 79 was a beautiful car. Unlike today's incarnations with their add-on accoutrements and unsightly aerodynamic appendages, the Lotus 79 decked out in the iconic black and gold of sponsors John Player was simple, sleek, uncluttered and frankly the most attractive Formula One car ever built, then and today. How the sport allowed a natural beauty to transform into the wizened witch of modernity is something to be regretted by all aficionados of motor racing.

Brabham's answer to the black-and-gold pace-setter came at the Swedish Grand Prix. Lauda and his team-mate John Watson had struggled for the early part of the campaign, but they knew that Murray had designed something quite special for mid-season and at Anderstorp it was unleashed to an unsuspecting paddock. Basically Murray had attached a fan to the rear of the car, mainly according to the engineer to cool the engine, but its effectiveness in creating the downforce that had been the sole domain of Lotus up until then was staggering. Both drivers were instructed to qualify on full fuel tanks so as not to warn their opponents of how fast the car would be, and in the race Lauda himself held back as much as he could behind Andretti's Lotus before the sheer speed of the car dictated that he took the lead and won the Grand Prix at a canter. £200,000 of development had gone into it a huge amount at the time but the furore that it caused amongst the other teams after the race meant that the car was never seen again. Up until recently it had always been thought that the FIA had banned the Brabham for being too dangerous, rightly surmising that if it had been in an accident, then a blade of the fan could shear away and cause serious damage and hurt to any following car and its driver, but it transpired that in fact Ecclestone had withdrawn it for political reasons. At that early stage, Bernie was looking at a bigger picture. Lauda only won one more race that season the ill-fated and tragic Italian Grand Prix at Monza.

The famous Brabham fan car-one race, one win and then withdrawn

James Hunt's career started to slide inexorably from 1978. Although the McLaren team's competitiveness was at its lowest for years, Hunt's performances in the car were not of Championship standard. Numerous accidents and lack-lustre drives meant that he scored just eight points throughout the season and finished 13th in the standings, even at times being out-raced by his new team-mate Patrick Tambay. There were the usual headline grabbing moments of course. He was fined $500 in Brazil for driving without a helmet after spinning in qualifying, and after another accident in Monaco, he celebrated the night away at the well-known 'Tip Top' bar. It ended with the Monagasque police charging the room with batons drawn and Jane Birbeck receiving a black eye in the process. He'd also hardly endeared himself to Jane earlier that weekend when he had told her they were going for some drinks at the Palace Hotel, only to arrive at Prince Ranier's Palace and poor Jane was unsuitably dressed for the occasion, much to her dismay. James of course wore his usual T-shirt and jeans.

No longer competitive, but Hunt still enjoyed himself Brazil 1978

Off the track his over-use of alcohol and substances started to affect his performance and team boss Teddy Mayer was now deeply concerned about his
driver's mental attitude. The women continued to drift in and out of his life
on a regular nightly basis, something which Jane Birbeck appeared to dismiss,
and it was clear that his love of motor racing was waning, and in turn its
love of him was fast receding too. A prime example was at Brands Hatch, the
scene of his triumphant 1976 victory, where he was idolised by the thousands
who attended. The author remembers seeing Hunt walking behind the main
grandstand on race-day, carrying a leather bag and shoeless (what chance of
that happening now hours before a Grand Prix?), completely ignored by the
fans. Their apathy toward the once great British hero was probably increased
after he crashed on the eighth lap whilst running in 13th place. There were
suggestions that Hunt was still under the influence of whatever substance he
had been taking the night before, but this was strenuously denied.

In Germany two weeks later he was nearly disqualified for 'brake-testing'
Vittorio Brambilla after passing him and believing the Italian had held him
up. It made him even more unpopular with the drivers and press alike and

by the time the Dutch Grand Prix arrived in August, he was so disenchanted that he seriously thought of retirement. If he had taken that decision, then few would have mourned his loss as he was now a shadow of his former self on the track and his excesses off it were no longer endearing. One thing changed his mind though, and that was a £1 million offer to join the Wolf team for the 1979 season. Hunt was financially secure by now and had invested in a night club in Marbella called 'Oscar's' named after his beloved Alsatian dog, but a million pounds is difficult to turn down. He even rejected an offer to drive for Ferrari, which seemed almost incomprehensible, although the thought of a free-will like Hunt driving for the political machine that was Ferrari seems inconceivable. Rejecting the criticisms of his decision and trying to prove that the move was not just for financial reward, he said: 'My aim is to be World Champion in 1979 so that I can go out of this business on a high'. They were brave and honourable words, but the Italian Grand Prix very nearly forced him to walk away completely.

The accident at the start of the 1978 Italian Grand Prix was one of the worst the sport has ever seen. When the green light came on, only a handful of cars at the front of the grid were stationary after the warm-up lap, whilst the ones at the back of the grid were still moving at some speed toward their positions. This concertina affect meant that some cars, Ricardo Patrese's Arrows amongst them, flew at speed at the first corner and there was just nowhere to go. In the melee that followed, Patrese, Hunt and the Lotus of Ronnie Peterson collided and cars smashed into each other, Hunt's briefly airborne. The Lotus burst into flames with Peterson trapped inside, whilst Brambilla's Surtees was wrecked with its driver unconscious with serious head injuries after being hit by a flying wheel. Hunt ran back to the Lotus and with the help of a marshal put out the flames, and then with Clay Regazzoni somehow managed to pull the Swede out of the car. Peterson's legs were badly broken but it seemed as if he was not as badly hurt as feared. Hunt returned to the motorhome white and ashen faced, trembling with fear. Peterson was one of his closest friends and had said that when he had looked into Ronnie's face as he lay on the track, he knew he was in trouble and the Swede was 'terribly frightened'.

The race restarted with Mario Andretti, in the lead Lotus, taking sixth place and the one point needed to win the World Championship. Hunt had driven at the back of the pack and retired with ignition problems, and then left Monza hurriedly. Earlier he had been persuaded by members of his new Wolf team, notably Harvey Postlethwaite and manager-to-be Peter Warr to take the restart, but it was clear he no longer had the appetite for the sport. He left the circuit as American Andretti celebrated his World Title, the first from the States since Phil Hill. Sadly the celebrations ended abruptly when the news came through that Ronnie Peterson had died in hospital after complications in the operation to save his legs. It was a huge shock as Peterson was one of the fastest and most popular of drivers and it seemed such an unnecessary accident to have. His funeral, in Orebro in Sweden, was attended by over 15,000 mourners, including Jody Scheckter, John Watson, Emerson Fittipaldi, Niki Lauda and James Hunt.

The aftermath saw the blame-game and it was deemed that Patrese, who had a reputation as being slightly arrogant and aggressive, was to blame and he was banned from the next Grand Prix. Hunt was particularly vocal in his criticism of the Italian and in fact spent the rest of his motor racing life, including his broadcasting career, complaining about his driving. Three years later Patrese was cleared of any wrong doing and he and the race starter, both of whom had been charged with manslaughter by the Italian authorities, were completely absolved of any blame. It was not enough for Hunt, who continued to criticise and castigate Patrese at every given opportunity, and some wondered whether his assassination of the Italian was in a way a sub-conscious effort to atone for any guilt he may have felt for the death of Peterson, as it was his car that veered into the Lotus and TV replays showed that in fact Patrese's Arrows had not touched the McLaren at all. Patrese went on to be one of the most successful Formula One drivers in terms of races started and became a respected figure within the sport. To the eternal credit of the Italian, he hardly showed anger or bitterness toward his early detractors for the rest of his career.

The Royal Swedish Automobile Club gave Hunt their prestigious Golden Shield for his bravery in rescuing Peterson, but Hunt was not a receiving hero. It did not sit easily with him as he made the point quite forcibly that he was the first driver on the scene and it was pure instinct. He believed that anyone in that situation would have done the same, and if nothing else, he was now viewed in a totally different light by the fans and press alike. Another thing was for certain too, the event changed his mindset completely and even the thought of one million pounds in his bank no longer kept alive his love of the sport.

As a footnote, it is interesting that the accident was not mentioned or even referred to in Lauda's autobiography 'To Hell and Back'. Instead he concentrated on the fact that he had won the race despite being given a one minute penalty for jumping the restart. Some might suggest a coldness, whilst others would point out the single and selfish resolve needed to be successful in an unforgiving career choice.

The season ended far too slowly for both. Lauda was desperate to get a more competitive car and Hunt was desperate to get out.

CHAPTER TWENTY ONE

Time for farewell

Hunt had said goodbye to the McLaren team, and despite their at times fractured relationship, he had left on good terms. At the final race of the season in Canada, the mechanics had stuck a note on his steering wheel which said: 'This is the last one buddy it's been a great three years'. He had been their most high-profile, and certainly most successful driver alongside Emerson Fittipaldi, since the team were formed and his loss was one they would struggle to overcome. In fact the team became totally uncompetitive for a number of seasons until the arrival, ironically, of a certain Niki Lauda in the early 1980s. Hunt prepared himself for a new challenge, racing for the Wolf team.

Walter Wolf was an Austrian, brought up in Canada and who had made a fortune in the oil industry. He lived the life of a very rich man and that included starting his own Formula One team in 1977. After hiring Harvey Postlethwaite to design a car, it astonishingly won its first Grand Prix in South Africa in the hands of Jody Scheckter and then scored two more triumphs that season to give its driver an outside chance of the Championship. Two years later, with Scheckter on his way to Ferrari, where he would become World Champion, the Wolf team were struggling.

Hunt had hoped that the 1979 season would be financially beneficial and also redeem himself on the track where he could at least show his competitiveness. The former was true, but the latter never came close. Hunt was no longer in love with the sport and admitted to his closest friends, including Jane, that he was now scared. He reckoned that if he got out of the sport, then he could reasonably expect to live to his 70s, whereas if he continued, then his life could end at any time. Too many people had died around him, and after the Ronnie Peterson crash, it was clear he no longer wanted a part of it all.

He was helped by a simply dreadful car that seemed to lurch from one crisis to another. In the first seven races of 1979, he had mechanical problems in six of them and struggled to finish in eighth in the other. After one particularly unpleasant moment at the South Africa Grand Prix in Kyalami where his brakes failed, he got out of the car and according to Jackie Stewart who was working for television at the time was 'a truly frightened man'. It took some powers of religious persuasion from Rob Walker (who was working with the Wolf team after spending years as a Formula One owner himself) to persuade James to sit in the car again. He basically told him that God would take care of him, which was enough for James to climb back into the cockpit. It was around this time though that he had made the decision that he had to get out of the sport, and after talking with Jane and his personal manager John Hogan, he decided to leave after the Monaco Grand Prix, the place where he had made his F1 debut six years previously.

Walking away, Hunt retires from F1

He kept it secret from the public and press alike, but once he'd managed to park the car against the Armco barrier, after the fourth lap of the race a drive shaft had broken to continue the car's unhappy record, he simply got out and walked away. No one blamed him, although a few questioned his ability, but the answer to that was that the man who replaced him in the Wolf team, Keke Rosberg, failed to make the car go any quicker or enjoyed too much success either that season. That spoke volumes as Rosberg was a 'coming' driver who went on to become World Champion a few years later.

Hunt said at the time: 'It comes as a great relief to stop racing and I look forward to relaxing for a while. I look forward to life after racing and I'm now taking a big step into a world that is unknown to me'. He obviously had no regrets about leaving a sport that was still as dangerous as when he first started, despite the numerous safety measures being introduced each year. He was financially self-sufficient and had made enough money to sustain him for the rest of his life, and he left Formula One after 92 Grands Prix, ten victories and a World Championship. The odd thing about James Hunt's motor racing career is that he won as many races in Formula One as he did in lesser Formulae, showing that his rise to the top was as unchartered as it was unusual. No other driver before or since has had quite a steep success curve without the experience to fall back on, unless you count Lewis Hamilton's recent McLaren-managed career. Hunt was and still is unique in so many ways.

His legacy had been summed up by Autosport's editor Quentin Spurring who said that Britain owed much to the talent that made Hunt World Champion in 1976, but nothing for the hooligan side of his nature that made him such a poor World Champion. Hunt certainly polarised opinion.

Niki Lauda had started 1979 in a similar frame of mind. Domestically life was bliss. His son Lukas was born and even though he missed the birth due to travelling in between races, actually on his way to Long Beach, it was inevitable that the responsibility of fatherhood would cloud his thinking when it came to motor racing. Of a far more pressing matter though was his passion for aeroplanes. After gaining his pilots licence, he had travelled everywhere in the air and in 1978 he had founded 'Lauda Air', a small company that would specialise in the routes abandoned by the mighty Austrian Airlines. It occupied his time, and as he was now a multi-millionaire, he could afford to fund it until it became self-sufficient. What he hadn't planned on was the intransi-gent attitude that Austrian Airlines had when discussing current and future routes for the fledgling business. It was obvious that this would take a lot of his time.

On the track, he started the season with Brabham and new team-mate Nelson Piquet and between them they managed to score points on just three occasions from twenty-eight starts, with Niki gaining a mere four points by the time the circus had arrived in Canada, round fourteen of the World Championship. The car was unwieldy due to the cumbersome and totally unreliable Alfa-Romeo engines, despite its stunning looks, and it became so frustrating that team owner Bernie Ecclestone dispensed with the Ital-ian company's services and reverted to the tried and trusted Ford Cosworth engines. By this time Lauda was seriously de-motivated and in a way of somehow proving his worth to Ecclestone, he demanded the extraordinary retainer of two million dollars for the 1980 season, a figure unheard of up to that time. Bernie would clearly not accede to such a request and negotiations went on for four months whilst both red cars ground to a halt on a depress-ingly regular basis.

Finally Ecclestone agreed and a contract was drawn up and signed, but in Montreal things changed. Lauda had won the battle, but he admitted after that it felt like a hollow victory and after getting into the new car and driv-ing it around for a few laps, he realised immediately that he too no longer wanted to be there. Whereas Hunt had planned his exit and had walked away gracefully, surprisingly for someone as graceless as Hunt, Lauda simply walked away. He spoke to Ecclestone, told him he no longer wanted to drive and caught the first flight to Los Angeles to talk to the McDonald aircraft factory. No one in the team knew and no one at the track was aware that the double World Champion had just quit. The first inkling came when experienced observers saw the Brabham, seemingly driven by Lauda, strug-gling way off the pace in practice.

Ecclestone had immediately agreed to release Lauda from his contract, feeling that he needed a driver who was committed to the cause, something that Niki no longer was. He then spotted the Argentinian Ricardo Zunino walking down the pit lane (there to watch the race in the hope of securing a full-time drive for the next season) and put him in Lauda's overalls and helmet which had been abandoned and told him to qualify the Brabham. By this time the Austrian was 30,000 feet in the air, and not for the first time had just walked away without a backwards glance. The two gladiators of 1976 were now absent from Formula One and immediately the sport was weakened by it.

CHAPTER TWENTY TWO

Life in the slow lane

With the absence of Hunt and Lauda, the world of Formula One kept turning, but arguably it was a poorer place. It was a time when the FISA/FOCA war broke out between the governing body (effectively represented by FISA who also had the turbo manufacturers alongside them such as Ferrari and Renault) and the English constructors (effectively FOCA who were run by the likes of Lotus, Williams and McLaren etc). It meant for battles throughout the 1980 and 81 seasons with Bernie Ecclestone (heading FOCA) and Jean-Marie Balestre (FISA) going head-to-head. It was unsavoury and painted the sport in a bad light with threats and counter-threats of breakaway Championships.

On the track, the personalities seemed to be missing. British fans had embraced the Williams team despite having an Australian Alan Jones as their number one driver and took to his World title in 1980 almost as if he had won it for Great Britain. The Williams team were patriotic in a Hesketh-sense, flying the union flag at every opportunity and so had replaced Lotus in the hearts of the British motor sports enthusiast. That must have been difficult to take for Northern Irishman John Watson, who had succeeded Hunt as the country's top driver, but his victory at Silverstone in 1981 was greeted with as much delight as Hunt's in 1977.

Lauda's departure from Formula One hardly registered in his home country as they were not a racing-mad community and in fact that year's Austrian Grand Prix was one of the more poorly-attended events on the calendar. Brabham had Nelson Piquet to spearhead their challenge, something he did with distinction, winning the first of his three World Championships in their car in 1981, while Ferrari returned to the crisis-led moments they had endured a decade earlier. After winning the driver's title in 1979 with Jody Scheckter, they produced one of their worst cars ever the following year and it needed the absolute brilliance of Gilles Villeneuve to give them any kind of competitiveness.

Niki Lauda didn't look back. He put all of his efforts into the new airline he had formed and spent most of the next two years living in hotels in Vienna whilst wife Marlene and son Lukas stayed in their house near Salzburg. His battles with Austrian Airlines were as tough as any he'd had on the track and it was clear that this was a battle that he just would not be able to win. He had initially invested around £200,000 in buying flying rights for smaller and shorter haul routes, using a 40-seater Fokker to fly holidaymakers south. It posed no threat to the huge Austrian Airline Corporation, yet they looked at Lauda as an unwelcome interloper and did everything in their power to destroy his company. If he laid on a route to an un-fancied destination, then they would do the same and immediately undercut the price. If he then pulled out of the route due to the competition, they too would then stop running it. It seemed as if there was no rhyme or reason to their assassination attempts on the Lauda Air organisation. In an attempt to fight back, Lauda bought a DC10 aircraft to offer a more upmarket option for his customers, taking on the Austrian Airlines head-on, but the ensuing recession and the hike in fuel prices meant it was a gamble that failed and the money, some £300,000, was lost. At one stage he met the Austrian Chancellor, along with the Transport Minister, Finance Minister and the Chief Executive of Austrian Airlines to try to find a resolution and thankfully the Chancellor Dr Kreisky made the point that the country of Austria had once driven a certain Mr Porsche into exile many years ago, and they didn't want to do the same to Herr Lauda. The uncertainty and confusion was not quite what he expected, and the amount of money having to be ploughed into the venture must surely have started to have some concern, but as he said: 'The money I poured into the business initially was not crippling, and neither were the subsequent periodic injection of funds. The amounts involved were never such as might endanger my future'. The facts were though that the huge fortune he had made from racing was disappearing fast literally into the skies.

His second child, Mathias, was born in 1981 and this time he wasn't 35,000 feet in the air when he heard the news, but thankfully just a few miles away in Salzburg. If this was likely to slow him down and if Marlene thought she had finally got her husband back to have a 'normal' life, then sadly she would be disabused of that notion. Niki's statement in his biography gave a telling insight into what was going on his mind: 'In essence not much had changed. The family stayed in Salzburg. I stayed on in Vienna. It was a curious period of transition. I believe we were all waiting for something to happen'. That 'something' was almost inevitable.

James Hunt had looked at retirement as a new way of living his life. He now craved the stability of a relationship and as well as attempting to have a baby with Jane, he proposed to her and they got engaged in November 1979. It was surprising to say the least, given his propensity for the opposite sex, but for a time James was changing. Jane suffered numerous miscarriages and the two decided that her constant travelling to and from London, where she worked, was a contributing factor. They also both realised that they actually hated Spain and having to spend more time there now that James wasn't travelling around the World was horrendous, despite the large British faction who lived there including actor Sean Connery who had become a close friend. They decided in spring of 1980 to return to Britain.

Financially James had never been better off, with a property trading company with his former manager Bubbles Horsley, the nightclub in Marbella and a huge squash complex in Munich. He was certainly a millionaire but was keenly aware that he had to make his money work to keep him in the lifestyle that he had enjoyed so much in the past. To that end, when he moved back to the United Kingdom, he invested in a renovated Mews House in London and bought a farm estate for £1 million. It was called Park Farm and included 590 acres with a six bedroom farmhouse, a stretch of river on the Great Ouse that had rights for coarse fishing and the lordship of the manors of Tyringham, Filgrave, Sherington and Emberton. The thought of James Hunt as a farmer seemed inconceivable and despite taking on the role with great enthusiasm, the fact that he hated fox-hunting, disliked riding horses and was hardly the gentleman esquire suggested that this was a flight of fancy instead of anything long-lasting. Sadly the same seemed to be said for his relationship with Jane.

They had arranged to get married, but she had resumed her career as a photographer's representative and had opened an agency in London. Soon she was offered a position with the IMG group run by Mark McCormack and simply decided to take the job as opposed to having the wedding. The tables had been turned on James and for once it was he who was being rejected. As she later said: 'We never talked of marriage again. It was just sort of quietly ignored. We missed our moment'

Sadly it went quickly downhill from then. In March 1980, James went on a skiing holiday in Verbier in Switzerland as a guest of a Marlboro sponsored team of skiers. After what he described as a 'major lunch', he went on to the slopes and had an accident that ruptured ligaments in his left knee. He was in hospital for weeks and had a plaster cast for nearly three months going through absolute agony. In typical James fashion, he attempted to rush the rehabilitation process and only delayed it with his exercise regime and caused himself further physical pain. That meant he became almost unbearable to live with, something Jane became more and more aware of.

The pain was so intense that even drugs, remedial and recreational, failed to ease his discomfort and at this point he simply stopped communicating with Jane on any level. She in turn, unsure as to how to help her partner, joined him in a spiral of drugs and alcohol, and as she said later: 'I felt he was just pulling me down'. She didn't visit him in hospital as much as was expected and it was clear that the relationship was unravelling. As Christmas approached she had another miscarriage and as the New Year dawned the inevitable happened. James still had a roving eye and in a tearful confession one evening, he opened up his feelings to her. Jane admitted she was distraught as the two were ready to part, as there was no way she could live with a partner who just could not be faithful, but the separation was amicable. They discussed their financial commitments with Bubbles Horsley as a mediator and James gave Jane the London house and agreed an allowance for her for six months. He even invested in an exercise club she was opening in Chelsea, and at one stage later in the year they tried a brief reconciliation. It lasted for about six weeks until as Jane put it: 'One night, he just didn't come back'. Jane eventually had a long term relationship with the athlete Daley Thompson and now very rarely, if ever, talks of her time with James. It was another sad ending to a seemingly happy unison for James.

His business world was also beginning to encounter problems and his farming plans, never the most solid of ideas, soon faded away. He sold Park Farm for about the amount he had paid for it, relinquished his share of the squash club in Munich, and now that he lived in London, soon sold off the nightclub in Marbella. In its place, he bought a rambling house on the edge of Wimbledon Common and proceeded to enjoy life in the only way he knew how.

CHAPTER TWENTY THREE

Back to F1

The McLaren team, struggling to re-establish themselves, approached Hunt at the start of the 1980 season and with sponsors Marlboro, offered him £1.4 million to return. Hunt turned it down, but was seriously considering making a one-off appearance at the Long Beach Grand Prix to replace newcomer Alain Prost who had hurt his wrist. Hunt asked for the ridiculous sum of £1 million for the weekend, but Marlboro offered half of that and it seems as if a deal was about to be done when James had his untimely skiing accident. A couple of years later, Bernie Ecclestone, now mindful of the sport losing most of its characters, tried to lure James back with a 16-race £2.6 million deal, but it too was rebuffed. Hunt no longer wanted to risk his life anymore and had become far more relaxed in his 'real' life outside of driving a car very fast. Ironically, in the race that James was prepared to return in, at Long Beach, Clay Regazzoni a veteran and highly experienced racer – crashed into a concrete wall and was left paralysed from the waist down. Maybe James was more astute than people gave him credit for.

Hunt did return to Formula One in 1980 though, as an analyst for the BBC alongside commentator Murray Walker. It came about after Hunt had joined the commentary team at Silverstone the previous year and had impressed the producer of the '*Grand Prix*' programme, Jonathan Martin. He had hired Hunt to sit alongside the vastly-experienced and conscientious Murray Walker, not that Walker was exactly overwhelmed by the prospect. Their first experience together was actually covering a Formula 5000 race at Silverstone, where James lay on the floor with his leg in plaster and his final comment after Murray had done most of the work was to describe the race as a 'load of rubbish'. It hardly endeared him to Walker.

Murray Walker had become an icon in sports broadcasting. In Britain certain voices are inextricably linked to the sports they are describing. Dan Maskell with tennis, Bill McLaren with rugby union, Eddie Waring with the league version, Peter Allis with golf, Harry Carpenter with boxing and Murray

Walker with motor racing, yet Murray's first love was motorcycling. His dad, Graham, was a European motorcycle Champion in 1924 and later became a commentator for BBC Radio. Murray, who also competed on motorcycles and lists the Isle of Man TT as one of the highlights of his year, did his first commentary in 1949 when standing in for his father. He continued this on a part-time basis whilst keeping down a very successful career in advertising. His agency was responsible for the famous slogan; 'A Mars a day helps you work, rest and play'.

His commentating duties became more involved and when the BBC started broadcasting highlights of Formula One in 1978, no coincidence that it was only two years after the famous Hunt/Lauda battle for the title, Murray made the programme his own. Up until that point most motor racing commentaries for the BBC were done by Raymond Baxter, but from the moment Murray Walker officially took over the microphone, he was the voice of Formula One in Britain and many countries where the coverage was aired.

James Hunt's arrival was not exactly welcomed by Walker who quite understandably was concerned that the BBC were looking to ease him out, instead of creating the chemistry that eventually seeped through their commentaries. He had known Hunt throughout his racing days and had hardly been impressed with his behaviour. As Murray has often said, he regarded Hunt as: 'the archetypal, loud-mouthed Hurray Henry' that he so disliked. The age difference obviously played a part, but Hunt's seemingly lack of commitment to his new job would certainly irk Walker in their early years. Stories have been told and retold of Hunt arriving late and asking Walker who was on pole (something which seemed to be done just to annoy Murray who had done extensive research with copious amounts of notes and statistics), or the time at his first official commentary in Monaco of arriving with a bottle of Rose wine, clearly the worse for wear and promptly planting his plaster encased leg on Murray's lap and gave his insightful analysis from that position.

Somehow the two of them gelled and their chemistry was a joy to listen to. Murray would commentate in his high-octane manner (perfect for the sport he was describing), whilst James would rather languidly offer his opinion on what had taken place, either praising a driver to the skies, or especially when it came to Ricardo Patrese, who he continued to ridicule at every opportunity question how they ever got into Formula One in the first place! Frenchman Jean-Pierre Jarier was another who was regularly on the receiving end of Hunt's blunt and pointed criticisms. As a way of attempting to keep the uncluttered flow going, they shared one microphone so as not to talk over each other. If James wanted to say something, he would simply tap Murray on the shoulder, something which he did far more regularly as the races and years passed.

Niki Lauda returned to F1 in 1981, but his was a far more involved process. The 'something' he had referred to was of course the racing bug that he had never really got out of his system. Add to that the fact that Lauda Air was haemorrhaging money, and Niki knew he had to do something to change matters. At first, after his retirement, he had hardly looked at a Grand Prix, but in mid 1981 he attended the Austrian GP as a summariser for Austrian TV to experienced broadcaster Heinz Pruller (the Walker/ Hunt of Austria), and interviewed the three drivers on the podium, Jacques Laffite, Rene Arnoux and Nelson Piquet. He enjoyed the experience and later in the month also attended the Italian Grand Prix at Monza. Soon he started to wonder if he could still do a reasonable job in a current Formula One car and with the help of his fitness guru Willi Dungl, made sure that physically he would be in a position to at least do himself justice. Dungl was at first sceptical and made Lauda cycle for miles and miles, but soon came to the conclusion that it could be done.

Ron Dennis had bought the McLaren outfit from Teddy Mayer in 1980 when the team's fortunes were at a low ebb, and with the help of designer John Barnard (who introduced a carbon fibre monocoque to the sport for the first time, meaning that the rigidity of the material would mean fewer sections were needed to build the car and so it would in effect be safer and certainly easier to streamline in the ground effect era), was preparing to unleash a new car and new team on the F1 world. Already rebuffed by James Hunt at the beginning of the decade, McLaren and sponsors Marlboro approached NIki Lauda about a possible comeback, and received a positive response. They wanted an experienced driver to replace the erratic Italian Andrea de Cesaris and bring back the success that the team had lost since the departure of James Hunt. Financial negotiations began and a retainer of

$2million dollars was agreed and so came the first test drive of the new car in secret.

The secrecy was so pervading that even Marlene his wife had no idea as to how serious it was. Niki took her to England and left her in London, whilst he travelled north to Donington Park, the 'rather odd circuit' as he described it, in the midlands. With the help of John Watson now a McLaren driver, a few mechanics and certainly no reporters, Lauda spent a few laps getting used to the new breed of Formula One car with bone-jarring suspension, ground effect technology and vastly-improved cornering speeds that gave incredible g-forces. Within three laps he had to come back into the pits, as it was clear to him, if no one else, that he didn't have the strength to drive one of these new cars for such a period of time, incredible how in just two years since he walked away, Formula One could have advanced so quickly, but that is what puts it at the pinnacle of technological achievement. Eventually he got to grips with the machine and lapped within a tenth of 'Wattie's' time. The speed was still there.

As is always the case at moments like this, offers suddenly come unexpectedly and Frank Williams contacted Lauda that very evening asking him to join his team as Alan Jones had announced his retirement, but Lauda had committed to McLaren and Ron Dennis in particular and so his decision was easy. What was not so easy was breaking the news to Marlene, who took it badly and denounced her husband as being 'mad'.

In between the test on the 16th September 1981 and the opening Grand Prix of the 1982 season, Lauda wracked up as many testing miles as he could and trained as hard as he could with Willy Dungl to be at his fittest since retiring. He was slightly overweight and his stamina was questioned, but the sheer single mindedness that made him such a great Champion meant that these things would be overcome by the time he returned to competitive action. Even a big accident whilst testing in France hardly registered on his upwards graph of progress. He had been taught by Dungl that after the car comes to a halt, sit quietly and breathe slowly, then get out and do the same again. At Le Castellet, when the McLaren sheered its rear suspension, he careered into the safety netting (long before run-off areas, the way of stopping a racing car at high speed was to have rows of safety netting held up by wooden poles, an improvement on straw bales and old tyres from previous eras but still hardly cutting-edge!), and fell apart as Lauda hit the barrier at around 180mph. Four minutes later Dungl arrived from the pits, held his wrist and took his pulse. It said 90. For most 'normal' people a crash like that would probably see a three figure number, but Lauda was not most 'normal' people.

The announcement that two-times World Champion Niki Lauda was returning to the sport was greeted with excitement and scepticism alike. Many observers questioned his desire after the antics of Canada in 1979 when he had just walked away without a backward glance or a farewell and many quite rightly believed that he was back for financial inducement as his airline was struggling, but others welcomed him with open arms. One was old friend James Hunt. As far as he was concerned, Niki was making the right decision: 'If he wants to race, it's because he wants to do it, because that's the sort of animal he is. Let's have Niki back'.

It's possible on the strength of Lauda's comeback that Hunt decided to take a more active role in the sport as well as his broadcasting duties. He became an advisor and tutor to up-and-coming Marlboro drivers, the most successful being a future World Champion in Mika Hakkinen. It meant that both Hunt and Lauda were still alive and kicking in Formula One. Lauda was back to what he did best, driving, whilst Hunt was doing something he was good at. If not driving anymore, he was giving his opinion on those who did.

CHAPTER TWENTY FOUR

Lauda in charge

Niki Lauda's return to Formula One could not have been any more dramatic. For the opening Grand Prix of the 1982 season, in South Africa in the last weekend of January, he organised a strike. When he had made his decision to return to the sport and proved to himself more than any other that he was fit enough to compete, he then had to go through the usual administration to be allowed to drive in a Formula One race. Despite being two-times World Champion, he still had to apply for a licence, a 'super-licence' for the elite drivers to compete at the pinnacle of their sport. This he did but was immediately perturbed as to the content. In the few years since his departure, things had changed and the licence gave far too much power to the teams, meaning that they in effect could decide whether a driver stayed with them or moved on, taking any authority away from the individual. For someone like Lauda, that was simply a red-rag to a bull.

He'd contacted Didier Pironi, who was at that time the President of the Grand Prix Drivers Association (GPDA) and eventually persuaded him that the contracts were not fair, and after then convening a meeting with the other 28 drivers, the two saw that in fact only five had signed them. The other 25 were required to do so before being allowed on to the track for qualifying but in a surprising force of solidarity (something very rarely shown in the sport – ask Jackie Stewart about his safety campaign!) all the drivers, except Jacky Ickx and Jochen Mass, agreed to boycott the opening practice session on Thursday. What followed was almost a 'carry-on' type farce.

Lauda and Pironi organised a coach and a chauffeur and then with all the drivers on board drove to a luxury hotel on the outskirts of Johannesburg, with reporters, TV crews and of course team managers in tow. There they hired a huge room, so that they could all stick together and not be separated during the evening, and proceeded to lock themselves away. The tedium was countered by piano playing from Gilles Villeneuve and far more elegantly by Elio de Angelis, whilst Lauda and Pironi soothed the nerves of the younger and more fragile drivers with words of support. All the time the team managers were literally on the other side of the door threatening immediate dismissal unless they climbed back into their cockpits and raced. Sponsors were unhappy and the news of a F1 strike led by Niki Lauda reverberated around the world.

The stand-off continued with Bernie Ecclestone standing alongside the FISA President Jean-Marie Balestre with their threats, and one team manager Mo Nunn of Ensign actually arrived with bodyguards and police to attempt to 'rescue' his young driver Roberto Guerrero. Only one deserted, Teo Fabi, and finally after complex negotiations at the track between Pironi and the circuit organisers, it was agreed that the race would go ahead as the 'super-licence' requirements would be waived. On the track in the race, Lauda finished a creditable fourth in his second F1 'debut'.

Afterwards there were threats of the drivers being arrested at the airport for not honouring their contracts to race, or they would be banned for life. Neither of these things happened, but FISA eventually fined each individual $5,000 for non-participation on Thursday, although each driver appealed. The money could be found by Lauda without a second thought, but some of the 'paying' drivers would have found it difficult. It was an astonishing weekend and one which F1 had not seen before, but it overshadowed the fact that Formula One was also still willing to race in a country that had been abandoned by the rest of the sporting world due to its apartheid laws. F1 doesn't always have a conscience.

In Brazil he collided with Reutemann but at the US (West) Grand Prix in Long Beach, he won. It was an incredible achievement to take his car to victory in only his third race back and silenced the loud and vociferous critics who had rounded on him even more after the events in Kyalami. He'd started alongside pole-man Andrea de Cesaris and waited for the inevitable mistake from the erratic Italian, and once passed, drove a simple and disciplined race to take the chequered flag. It was a dream come true and he enjoyed every second of it. As he said in his autobiography, published four years later: 'I was shouting and whistling for joy. Then I thought, watch yourself, you idiot, just watch yourself, otherwise you'll drive into the wall out of sheer stupidity. I have never felt like that before. It was beautiful'.

A return to F1 and Lauda wins his third race!

Lauda had defied all the critics, of which there were many, and there was no doubt in his mind that he could now win a third World Championship. It wouldn't come in 1982 as the McLaren was not the competitive car that was needed and that was shown in the next few races. He did manage to finish third at Zolder in Belgium, but was disqualified after it was found his car was underweight by 1.8 kilos a race his team-mate John Watson won and a race that saw the wonderfully talented and charismatic Gilles Villeneuve killed in a needless qualifying accident. Villeneuve had arrived in Belgium in emotional turmoil after his Ferrari partner Pironi had taken victory at the previous Grand Prix in San Marino, effectively ignoring team orders and taking away a certain win for Gilles. Whatever caused the accident, whether mechanical or driver-error, it deprived the sport of one of its greatest talents and the 'what-might-have-been' question is forever on every motor racing fanatic's lips.

Sadly the accidents and fatalites didn't end in 1982 in Formula One. Ricardo Paletti was killed at the Canadian Grand Prix, and Championship pacesetter Didier Pironi was seriously injured in qualifying for the German Grand Prix at Hockenheim. He suffered terrible injuries to his legs and never raced again. The race for the title was between Lauda's team-mate John Watson and

Keke Rosberg, with the Finn taking it at the last race of the season around a car park in Las Vegas of all places despite only winning one Grand Prix all season. Lauda finished fifth, which included a comfortable win at the British Grand Prix at Brands Hatch, but he did suffer a badly damaged wrist at the aforementioned German Grand Prix after crashing heavily in practice. The season had been both successful and disappointing for the Austrian. He had won two races, which had surprised many, but it was clear the car was not going to be as competitive as he'd hoped, as the turbo-era was now in full swing and McLaren were now looking for a partner who could supply an engine.

James Hunt continued his erratic but compelling commentaries for the BBC, and in September of 1982 he met a new love, Sarah Lomax. She was 24, eleven years younger than James, and was initially flattered that he paid more attention to her than anyone else at a beach party in Spain whilst she was on holiday. He then pursued her when she returned to England and after dating for a few months, he showed his commitment by travelling to Washington regularly to spend weekends with her as she had now moved to America to work for an interior decorating firm. He also bought her a bicycle as she had a seven mile journey to work each day, although she was probably hoping for something a little more up-market. On one of his visits there, he proposed and she accepted. At first she was quite overwhelmed by his attention, even though friends had warned her about him. She knew little about his racing-exploits and her dream of a happy life was a happy man and a contented family home. It seemed at first as if that was exactly what James wanted too, but to be fair and accurate about Sarah, she also knew how to party. She had been brought up in a rectory in Wiltshire but had rebelled later at boarding-school. After a debutante month, she then ran off to Corfu for a while and worked in a selection of bars, before attempting to settle down. It seemed meeting James was simply a match made-in-heaven.

On the 17th December 1983 they married at a registry office in Marlborough, Wiltshire, this despite James being late and without a tie, his brother Peter had to quickly commandeer one before the ceremony could take place. They moved into James' huge Wimbledon home and proceeded to enjoy all that life could throw at them. The parties were noisy and raucous and went on beyond late and at times beyond early the next morning. They loved each other and referred to the other as 'Beast', hardly the most romantic of terms, but it seemed to describe their lifestyle and relationship. Sarah later said that James thought he had married a 'wild, drug-taking sex maniac'. She seemed perfect for him.

Running the Hunt household was a man called Winston. He was a Jamaican taxi driver who James had connected with one day when asking the driver to speed up as he was inevitably late for a meeting. Winston was stopped by the police and then lost his licence, so James immediately felt responsible and hired him as a gardener, chauffeur, chef and general houseman. Winston was eccentric to say the least, but became a loyal and trusted friend, often chasing journalists away from the house when they came to inquire after another Hunt-misdemeanour.

The house was a haven of pleasure. There was a games room with a full-scale snooker table which James and friends would play on for hours getting progressively more and more drunk. In the garden there was another instrument of a latest passion, a golf net where he could practice his swing daily. Since his bad knee injury, tennis and squash were out of the question, so golf and snooker became the new addictions. Amongst the partying and games, there was also evidence of a different James Hunt, a kinder and more sensitive side. His beloved Alsatian dog Oscar was always by his side, almost like a father-son relationship at times. There was an African Grey Parrot called Humbert who had been with the family for years, and tales, which have probably been embellished down the years, are told of how it disgraced itself at a Christmas Production of '*Treasure Island*' at the Mermaid Theatre where it had won the 'starring' part. Instead of saying the predictable 'pieces of eight', it repeated over and again something far less family-friendly. There was also a huge budgerigar collection, a throwback to a passion that James had when he was a child. One of his earliest ambitions was to breed the birds and then make a fortune by selling them after they had won numerous awards. It didn't quite work out that way when he was a child, but the passion continued to burn brightly, and his love of the birds became a serious commitment after he retired from racing. There was no doubt that James Hunt at times could be a contradiction within himself.

Life seemed good for him. It was quieter, and the only controversy he seemed to attract now was when he criticised other drivers on the television, but he looked outwardly to be a man that was at peace with himself. Sadly the demons that had plagued him, were beginning to take control as his life started to spiral downwards.

CHAPTER TWENTY FIVE

Lauda gambles his future

Niki Lauda renegotiated his contract for 1983 and became arguably the best paid driver ever in Formula One up until that time. It was galling for team principal Ron Dennis, but Lauda was the hottest property in a pretty barren market, so he had little choice but to acquiesce to his demands. For Lauda it was a personal triumph, but he must have looked to the new season on the track with a certain amount of dread. The turbos were rampant, particularly with Renault, Ferrari and Brabham-BMW, and the normally-aspirated brigade (ie, those who used the tried and trusted Ford-Cosworth engines) were left trailing some way behind. Thankfully McLaren were a forward thinking organisation and Ron Dennis had already approached Porsche about building them a turbo engine. The German company were not big fans of F1, preferring to compete very successfully in long distance sportscar events. They said they would build it if someone else would pay, so Ron Dennis than approached the main sponsor of Williams, TAG, and persuaded them that being a part share owner of a team was better than just having your name emblazoned on the side of a car. It was typical Dennis business dealing with a big help from Lauda, both as an ambassador for the team and as a personality, actually being the conduit between the two when tensions ran high due to extra demands when arranging the contract.

It was clear that the car needed the engine, despite the opening two races of the season being quite successful. In fact at Long Beach John Watson and Niki Lauda finished first and second, but they had qualified twenty second and twenty third! Numerous accidents and retirements helped their cause, but also some quite audacious overtaking manoeuvres meant that Watson created a record of the lowest grid position winning an F1 race. At Monaco two months later, the team reached an all-time low. In front of all of their sponsors, not just the huge contingent representing Marlboro, but the ancillary names that made up the budget that ran a top class Formula One team, and at the most prestigious and glamourous Grand Prix, maybe even sporting event, in the world, both cars failed to qualify. In those days practice times from each day were taken for the grid positions and on Thursday they had major tyre problems and on Saturday it rained. For the first time in ten years Niki Lauda had failed to qualify for a Grand Prix and the sight of the two Marlboro-McLarens sitting almost forlornly in the pit lane was something few observers expected. The turbo engine was needed and quickly.

There then followed a typical Lauda versus the rest scenario. The Porsche engine would not be ready until the end of the year, and McLaren designer John Barnard wanted to build a new car around the engine, but Lauda argued that the unit should be used the moment it was available so that any teething problems could be sorted before the start of 1984, instead of having those problems and niggles take away a possible Championship-charge. He had already sacrificed a full season as 1983 brought about a total of two podium finishes in the opening two races of the season, and was not willing to do it again. As it was obvious that Bernard and especially Dennis were not keen on bringing the project forward, Lauda did what he always did in situations like this. He got his own way.

He simply went to sponsors Marlboro, told them what they were missing out on and they in turn put enourmous pressure on McLaren to install the engine as soon as it was ready. The scheming infuriated Ron Dennis and the relationship between driver and team manager detioriated badly. It didn't matter much to the Austrian as he now had a car that, once it blew up a few times in the last Grands Prix of the season, would be ready to take control of the 1984 World Championship. To confirm Dennis's anger with Lauda, when the car first went testing in Germany with the new engine installed, it was with John Watson behind the wheel and not the man who had instigated its arrival. Dennis was also angry that Porsche had earlier tested the engine in one of their sportscars and had to remind them forcibly that in fact he and TAG were paying for an engine that was exclusive to McLaren.

All of this was playing behind what turned out to be a quite disastrous season for the team and its drivers despite the Long Beach success. Sadly for Watson and Lauda the end of 1983 soured dramatically. Watson, who had been at McLaren for a number of years, decided to stall on his contract talks, rightly believing that his results from the season where he had beaten the highly-paid Lauda comfortably meant that he was worth a lot more than the team were offering. Clearly Dennis was not prepared to pay any more than the driver's worth, especially after the way that Lauda had arranged his huge financial deal, and so when Renault released the fast up-and-coming driver Alain Prost, he pounced. Watson was no longer required and Frenchman Prost was installed as the number two. It was a desperate blow for the Northern Irishman and the same for the Austrian too. Lauda had always enjoyed working with Watson, rightly believing that although he was fast, he knew he could beat him at any time. He was the ideal number two driver. Prost was different. He was making a name at the French team before being released in rather unusual circumstances, and he was fast. At times, he was too fast. Add to that the fact that he wasn't going to cost anything like the amount that Lauda did and of course Niki was hardly flavour-of-the-day with Ron Dennis, then 1984 would be a far tougher season than he'd envisaged.

CHAPTER TWENTY SIX

Another title

If Niki Lauda thought that he would have serene progress to this third World Championship in what became very quickly the best car on the grid, then he would soon be disabused of that notion. His team-mate, unlike the compliant of the past, was not about to take second best just because Lauda was twice World Champion, and he was fast. In fact in qualifying he was consistently faster than Niki and outqualifed at virtually every race. He didn't have Lauda's guile and experience in those early days and when the race got underway, it was clear that the Frenchman still had a lot to learn, but he was a quick learner!

At first, Lauda's suspicion of Prost meant for a tense atmosphere within the team, but he soon warmed to him and realised that in fact there was a talent that was about to be unleashed and all Lauda could do was to stack the odds in his favour by testing the car to its maximum and getting as much information as possible for that extra edge. The new car was clearly going to be at the front of the grid, something which McLaren had struggled to do for some time, and this was Lauda's only real opportunity to take that third World Crown.

In the opening race in Brazil, it was despair though as Niki's engine, running as smoothly as hoped for, let him take a sizeable lead from the similarly turbo-powered Renault of Derek Warwick with Prost third, before it coasted to a halt at the mid-point. A battery cable had come loose, and to compound the sense of frustration, Prost had taken the win after an audacious passing manoeuvre on the yellow French car. Despite all of the pre-season testing and the scheming and politics that Lauda had employed to get the car and the team to his advantage, it was the new man, Alain Prost, who took McLaren's first turbo engine victory. Just as importantly it put him high on Ron Deniss's radar and the warmth that had eminated from the team manager since the protracted contract negotiations towards his 'number one' driver likened to an Arctic winter was cooling rapidly.

Lauda got his 'revenge' a fortnight later in South Africa where he won the Kyalami race, with Prost making a remarkable comeback from the back of the pack to finish second. After two races, the 'turbo-era' was seeing the re-emergence of McLaren as the team to beat with two remarkably competitive and closely matched team-mates.

The 'Turbo–era' was a crazy time when from 1977 at the British Grand Prix at Silverstone - Renault first introduced their car, powered by an in-house turbocharged engine as opposed to a naturally-aspirated engine that every other team used, and at first it was ridiculed for its slow responsiveness and a predeliction for blowing up in a spectacular way. Eventually they mastered its intricacies and soon the turbos were winning races and every team had to have one. By the time of the early 80s the cars were producing astronomical horsepower meaning ever-increasing speeds and at one stage teams were actually producing qualifying engines that would last for the duration before expiring, but only after putting its driver on pole position at a speed and a time that would previously have been unheard of. The g-forces that a driver had to deal with meant that they were now super-fit athletes and the sport was changing beyond recognition from the one that Lauda and Hunt had entered many years previously. To give an idea of the progress, Lauda's March that he drove in 1974 produced 400 horsepower, quite respectable and with the advent of the new aerodynamics, meant only the best could drive and handle a Formula One car at speed. By the time the McLarenMP4E hit the track, powered by the grunt of a Porsche turbo engine, the horsepower had reached 1000. This is what Lauda had to say about the turbo engine:

'Eventually, the whole procedure gets on top of you. As you accelerate, you find you can't shift fast enough to keep up with the tight rpm interval and the sudden turbo surge. You are slammed up against the rev limiter literally: as the revs build up, the turbo kick forces your head back, then you hit the limiter and your head is jolted forward, then you shift gear and your head is yanked backwards again, and so on three times in a row'.

That came from one of the most talented and bravest racing drivers there has ever been, writing in his autobiography in 1986. They were spectacular to watch and the speeds were quite phenomenal, but in an age when safety was becoming of paramount importance, they were clearly unsustainable. Formula One has always existed as the cutting edge of the latest technology with the unspoken remit of allowing any new advancement to eventually drip down to the road cars that we see in the showroom. That is the idea, but it is also a fiercely competitive sport and the reason why people are involved is simply to win. If a new idea ie aerodynamics, ground effect, fan assisted engines, turbos can give an extra advantage, then any team will spend its sponsors' money to develop those ideas. Ron Dennis always said of his McLaren team that they 'existed to win' and in 1984 that is exactly what they were doing.

Lauda's forunes waned in the next two races with mechanical retirements at Zolder and Imola for the Belgium and San Marino Grands Prix respectively. At the same time, Prost won in Imola and he headed the Championship, showing that the McLaren was now the car to beat as it had won three of the four races already. At Dijon-Prenois, a curious circuit that played home to the French Grand Prix, Lauda was determined to give a good showing so as not to be overshadowed by the inevitable clamour for a French, and on this occasion, a Prost win. Many observers had noted that Niki's driving style had changed and had become more aggressive in the race, maybe to make up for the disparity in speed to his team-mate over the qualifying period, and the fact that he had inevitably had to make up places from a poor grid position. This was never more obvious than in France.

He'd qualified ninth and trailed Prost in the race as the Frenchman showed all of his class and ability in front of an adoring and partisan crowd, before Alain avoided a huge accident when one of his wheels came loose. He pulled into the pits and out of the race. There was then a battle with the Renault of Patrick Tambay (a French driver in a French car, what could be better at Dijon?) and all of Lauda's experience and guile and bravery was needed as he harried and pressured the yellow and black car until Tambay made a mistake and Lauda was through to record his second win of the season. His delight didn't seem to be shared by Ron Dennis though. With Lauda's desire to overtake Tambay, he had uncharacteristically ruined his tyres and had been waiting for a signal from the pit lane to tell him to come in and change. In the pre pit-to-car radio days, the only way of communicating during the race was to make hand signals each time a driver roared past the pits, and in turn the pit mechanics would hang out a pit board with basic information such as placing, time ahead of the next car and which lap they were on. Before this race it had been agreed that the team would 'call' Niki's car in halfway through the race to replace the worn tyres, but no such message was shown on the pit board, and Lauda had to make the decision himself. As he said in his autobiography:

'I was really angry with Ron Dennis because he hadn't respected our halfway agreement. Taking unnecessary risks is always stupid. Never mind, that was the French Grand Prix, when 70,000 spectators saw Niki first and Renault second'

It hardly helped the atmosphere in the garage, and that cold front would be felt again at Monaco two weeks later.

The 1984 Monaco Grand Prix would surely not be run in this day and age. It was one of the wettest days the Principality has ever experienced and how the Formula One drivers of their day managed to keep the 1,000 horse power turbo engined cars on a track that quite simply would never be passed by any motor sport health and safety inspector if it was being designed for modern usage is as much a mystery as a marvel. The track remains because of its heritage and its glamour. It would never, ever be passed today if those things did not exist, with no run-off areas, guardrails inches from the track, hardly any overtaking areas and spectators barely three yards away from screaming cars struggling to reach treble figures in terms of speed due to the close confines.

Prost took pole with Lauda down in eighth, but in morning practice, he was much faster. It was then that he realised that Ron Dennis was seemingly on the side of Prost as the look of consternation on the team principal's face gave every indication. The garage was now becoming effectively two teams, although the drivers had become firm friends and colleagues.

The race saw numerous cars sliding and slipping. Briton Nigel Mansell led briefly in his Lotus only to throw away a certain victory after sliding on a white line painted on the road and planting his car into the barrier. The reaction from his boss, Peter Warr, now in charge of the team after the sad and untimely death of founder Colin Chapman, has been well-documented, but it was fair to say that Warr was not a member of the Nigel Mansell fan club. It has been reported that Warr said that his driver had just 'reached the extent of his very limited ability', but whether that was a mischief or correct quote, it showed how the future World Champion was perceived in the new Lotus set-up.

Lauda crashed whilst in second place. It was a moment of driver error and lack of concentration, and made even worse by the knowledge that Prost went on to win his third Grand Prix of the season, but tempered somewhat by the fact that only half points would be awarded due to the race being stopped before halfway as the conditions were now impossible.

It was the race where a new star was recognised on a global scale as Ayrton Senna produced a masterclass of wet-weather driving that showed him to be a future World Champion. Driving the unweildly and uncompetitive Toleman, he actually passed Prost as the flag was waved by official race steward Jacky Ickx (former F1 driver who was still having huge success in Sportscar racing), but as the result had to be back-tracked to the end of the previous lap, Prost was given the victory in a French principality with Senna second. The controversy that followed was typical of F1 with many observers believing that Ickx had taken favour with Prost, but the facts were he was simply applying the rules.

Also what has been overlooked down the years following Senna's incredible achievements in his short career was that on the day in Monaco, a certain German named Stefan Bellof was also providing a driving lesson to some of the other experienced names in his equally uncompetitive and naturally-aspirated Tyrrell. He was catching both Senna and Prost and could easily have won if the race had carried on. Bellof was killed some years later in a Sportscar event and it was another case of what-might-have-been as he was easily one of the most talented drivers to have reached Formula One by the 80s. As Germans Michael Schumacher and Sebastian Vettel are lauded by their compatriots for their achievements, one can only wonder as to what Bellof could have achieved.

There was a second place in Montreal but two poor races in Detroit and Dallas where no points were scored, but by the time of the British Grand Prix at Brands Hatch, the McLaren pairing were one and two in the World Championship. The 1984 season was one of the more curious ones in terms of points-scoring endeavours, as the powers-that-be had for reasons only known to themselves introduced a system where they divided the season into two halves and drivers could only take a certain amount of points from each half ie, their best results and drop the other points. It sounded complicated and became more so especially as Prost and Lauda were so dominant. It meant that if one driver recorded more victories in a season, but most were in one half, it was entirely possible that after the points had been calculated then he may not win the title. As it was, that is exactly what happened in 1984.

Brands Hatch was a triumph for Lauda as he recorded his third win of the season with the other Championship challengers, Prost and Nelson Piquet in the Brabham, both retiring, but his relationship with Ron Dennis hit a new low. Realising this could jeapordise any title hopes, Lauda acted and invited Dennis and his girlfriend Liza to Ibiza for a lazy day on the sea in Niki's boat. They talked things over and according to Lauda it was clear there was a love-hate feeling from Dennis, especially as he felt he had been blackmailed over the amount of money he was forced to pay Niki when there were few other options available at that time. Dennis also suggested there was little warmth from Lauda toward him, something which irked him bearing in mind how much he was getting paid. Lauda's feeling was that he wasn't being paid to be warm, but to be a very good racing-driver.

It seemed as if the meeting had gone well, but as they approached land for a meal at a restaurant, Dennis then announced that the next contractual offer to Lauda would be for exactly half of what he was paying now. The pleasant afternoon was ruined as there was no way that Niki would agree to having his salary halved, even if he acknowledged privately that he was being paid too much.

Not long after Lauda contacted Renault about a possible drive for 1985. He met the team manager Gerard Larrousse and at first negotiations stalled as it didn't look like the French team were interested in changing drivers, but the possibility of having a twice, and possibly three times, World Champion in their team became too tempting. Eventually a contract was presented, but Lauda rightly decided to hold off signing until another title was won. Despite the secrecy surrounding the meeting Lauda hadn't told anyone about it, Ron Dennis found out and immediately began to pressurise Niki into signing his contract. There were threats, games and politics aplenty and at one stage two hours before the start of the Austrian Grand Prix Dennis, according to Lauda, threatened to sign Keke Rosberg for 1985 unless Lauda put his signature to a contract there and then. It seems an unlikely scenario as Dennis is the ultimate professional and has only ever wanted his team to win, and so to jeapordise that by playing mind-games with one of his drivers just before an important Grand Prix looks counter-productive.

The Austrian Grand Prix showed Lauda at his cunning best. He had qualified fourth behind Piquet (his sixth pole of the year proving how fast, but unreliable the Brabham had become) with Prost and the Lotus of Elio de Angelis ahead of him. Piquet raced away, but after 28 laps De Angelis retired with an engine spewing oil and various bits all over the track. The unfortunate Prost then spun on the oil, not helped by the fact he was driving with one hand as the other was holding the gear lever in place as it had come loose at the start of the race. That left Lauda chasing Piquet looking for his first home Grand Prix victory in his career. With fifteen laps remaining he caught and passed the Brazilian, but then with a few laps left, there was a huge bang from the gearbox. Lauda coasted and was ready to retire, but as he didn't fancy walking back to the pits (he was on the other side of the circuit) he looked for a gear that worked so as to at least coast to retirement and save the unnecessary walk. He found that third, fifth and sixth gears were still working so he continued moving and was able to keep at a respectable speed, albeit five seconds per lap slower. It would only be a matter of time before Piquet overtook surely, but the Brabham didn't get any closer.

It was revealed after the race that Piquet's tyres were badly damaged and the Brazilian was convinced that Lauda was conserving fuel by slowing down and so he too had readjusted to a slower pace, believing that if he pressured Lauda, then the McLaren would simply pull away and the Brabham's tyres would probably not last the race. Lauda won the Austrian Grand Prix almost by default, and took great delight in telling Piquet how he had driven with just three gears for the last few laps. The Brazilian, who had only won twice all season despite setting pole positions and fastest laps, had thrown away a certain victory. It was a psycholigical blow and one that Lauda had delivered with consummate ease. Piquet's face on the podium, standing on the second step as opposed to the top where he should have been, tells its own story.

Lauda won in Italy, much to the disgust of the local fans who had now dismissed him after he had left Ferrari all those years ago, and finished a distant fourth to Prost's win in Germany. He'd also managed second places to Prost's firsts at Hockenheim (the European Grand Prix) and Zandvoort, Holland. It meant going into the last round of the World Championship, at the new circuit of Estoril in Portugal, Prost and Lauda had won eleven of the fifteen races and the Austrian led the Frenchman by just 3.5 points, knowing that second place would be enough to secure his third World Championship no matter what his team-mate did.

The Renault contract was never signed. The employees of the car giant heard about the huge amount of money ready to be paid and the unions had demanded it scrapped. It was a time when there were serious financial problems in the company, and a multi-million dollar deal was seen as almost obscene when workers were being laid off. It left Lauda with a problem. Dennis would not budge on his offer and had already contacted Rosberg, who seemed eager to join, so Lauda again did what he had to. He went to sponsors Marlboro and asked what they thought he was worth. They agreed to his demands and a new contract, about two thirds of what he had been paid before, was written and signed before the Championship showdown at Estoril. Lauda had got his way, now he just needed to do the same in Portugal.

The Portuguese Grand Prix had been re-instated onto the Formula One calendar, but the Estoril circuit was an unknown quantity. It was set amongst the dusty hillsides and seemed to be a well-made and challenging circuit, but hardly anyone came. The weather didn't help as it rained constantly on Saturday, but Portugal was neither a rich country nor a particularly interested one when it came to F1 in the 80s. So it came to pass that the World Championship decider would be played out in front of empty grandstands but a willing and excitable television audience.

The drama had started in qualifying where Prost has put his car second on the grid, but Lauda had a true nightmare and could only qualify eleventh. It could not have been much worse, but the old head on his shoulders reminded him that he only needed to finish second if Prost was to win the race to become Champion, but of course he had to pass nine cars to do that!

Prost pulled away into the lead and Lauda just bided his time, so much so that at mid-distance, he was still in eighth position. His best friend on the circuit, Nelson Piquet, would be more than willing to help Lauda's title charge now that his own challenge had ended, but he had somehow contrived to spin his Brabam early on and was nowhere to be seen. Lauda had particular difficulty in passing the Toleman of Stefan Johansson, mainly because the TV cameras were focused on Lauda's struggles and the Swedish driver was enjoying the spotlight, plus the fact that the Swede was a talented driver who had a long and successful career ahead of him. Eventually Lauda got through after a rare mistake from Johansson and then set about passing cars lap by lap. Soon he was closing in on the Lotus of Nigel Mansell in second, but the Briton was inspired and seemed to have a podium place in his grasp, some forty seconds clear of the McLaren and now pushing for the lead. Sadly for him, but to the delight of Lauda, his tyres gave way and the ensuing retirement put Niki Lauda in 'three-times World Champion' position.

When the chequered flag was waved, Lauda wasn't sure where he had finished, even shrugging his shoulders to Piquet as they slowed down together, but soon he got the word that he had finished second and was the 1984 World Champion. Two years after returning to the sport, he had won his third World Crown and it was an unusually emotional Lauda on the podium who hugged his team mate and promised that he would make sure that next season would be Prost's season.

Lauda wins title for the third time!

There was a great deal of sympathy for the Frenchman. He had won seven races to Lauda's five, but the peculiarity of the points system had given the title to Lauda. He had outqualified his team mate at virtually every race, but had been wanting when tactical awareness was needed. It was clear though that Prost had everything needed to become a great Formula One driver something which he eventually did by winning four World titles and the second highest number of Grand Prix victories in history.

On the podium also was Nikki's wife Marlene. She hadn't attended a race since the terrible accident in Germany in 1976, and had developed an absolute hatred of motor racing, but she wanted to be there to see her husband realise his dream. The hug she gave him whilst covered in the celebratory champagne was a defining image in the story of Niki Lauda's career.

After the three hours of interviews, by which time the virtually empty circuit was now completely deserted, Niki, Marlene and Willi Dungl (his loyal and brilliant fitness guru) attended a party hosted by sponsors Marlboro. Lauda handed out gifts to his mechanics and they all danced the night away in celebration of a dramatic but ultimately successful season all but two. Marlene complained of being unwell, so she and Niki retired to their hotel room and were in bed, perfectly sober, by half past midnight. The differences between the 1976 and 1984 celebratory evenings could not be starker. Whereas back in 76 when Hunt won his World Championship, he arrived back at Heathrow airport still quite drunk and had the embarrassing prospect of thousands of fans clamouring for his autograph and a chance to snatch a quick photograph with the new British sporting hero. When Niki Lauda arrived back in Austria, he returned home and then attended a pre-arranged television interview in a perfectly sober and sensible manner. There were the polar opposites that defined Hunt and Lauda. Hunt enjoyed his success to excess, almost as if he believed it could never come again, whereas Lauda took it all as part of his life. It had happened. He had won. Now the next one.

CHAPTER TWENTY SEVEN

Hunt into despair

James Hunt became a father for the first time on 12th September 1985 when Sarah gave birth to a boy, Tom, prematurely at St Theresa's hospital in Wimbledon. Tom weighed five and a half pounds and James was delighted, saying that he had lived for 37 years without responsibility but now of course things would have to change. Sadly they didn't.

To prove this, Hunt committed a stupid and childish act on a flight with British Airways to the Australian Grand Prix at the end of the year. He had been taking advantage of the free beer made available in first class and had then dozed off, only to awaken with an urgent need of the toilet. As they were all engaged he simply relieved himself against the curtain that separated first and economy class. It caused mayhem, not least with TV presenter Esther Rantzen who was also in first class, and once the newspapers got the story in Britain, Hunt was vilified by all. Headlines such as 'Hunt for Relief' and 'Going on the Boeing' may have made light of the unseemly episode, but it was the one incident in Hunt's life that turned the tide against him. Hardly any of his friends saw the funny side and one of his closest, 'Bubbles' Horsley (now a godparent to Tom) was singularly unimpressed and said so in no uncertain terms to Hunt.

Hunt's antics had once delighted the sporting world as he had been the original rebel, but now his behaviour was deemed as tiresome and childish. He had tired of his fame some time ago, and now fame was tiring of him. He was criticised for the incident, and of course every other misdemeanour was now remembered and analysed by the popular press. James was actually contrite and apologetic, especially to the airline and the passengers, but his actions were the much-used 'cry for help' as he was now drinking heavily and his marriage to Sarah was in trouble. Despite just giving birth, James seemed to expect his wife to continue partying like before, but like any other new mother, all Sarah wanted to do was to look after her firstborn. She was changing as a person with the new responsibility of parenthood, whilst James even though he loved his son dearly wasn't. In fact James was spiralling into a depression that was fed by drink, drugs and heavy partying and very soon the onset of severe financial problems.

Niki Lauda meanwhile was dealing with his own demons on the track as he tried to defend his World Championship. The new McLaren was competitive, but seemingly only for the one that had the number two painted on its nose cone. Prost, now desperate to win the crown that he inwardly felt was his the previous year, was in sensational form, winning the opening Grands Prix in Brazil, Imola (although he was later disqualified due to the car being underweight, something which is a recurring theme in the history of the team), Monaco and Silverstone. Lauda was trailing badly and after the British Grand Prix had finished in the points once and trailed in seventeenth place in the World Championship with just three points. He had retired in Brazil and Portugal (where the brilliant Ayrton Senna recorded his maiden Grand Prix victory in wet conditions driving the Lotus) and Monaco and it was in the Principality that he came close to quitting once again.

On the Thursday evening after the opening practice session, Lauda spoke to Keke Rosberg privately about the sport they were in and whether any of it was worthwhile anymore. Rosberg was highly rated and a former World Champion, yet he too had doubts about driving the ridiculously overpowered machines, at speeds and g-forces that literally left no room for error. Niki felt relieved that another driver had similar feelings. As he said: 'It was madness zooming around here (Monaco) like so many trained chimpanzees, 1,000 horsepower on this circuit. Madness' He had clearly fallen out of love with the sport, although mindful of the way he had walked away before, decided to give it some time and thought before making the final decision. The race in Monaco must have helped that decision as he spun on oil and the engine gave up. Another retirement.

It continued. Whilst his team-mate racked up the points as he charged toward a World title, Lauda struggled with unreliability and possibly little motivation too. In Canada he qualified seventeenth and even had time to stare into a beaver's eyes on trackside as he raced past, something he mentioned to Ron Dennis later. Dennis apparently smiled indulgently as it was the kind of moment that would not have taken place with the old-Lauda, but now that all efforts in the garage and team were being directed towards Prost, then lip-service was the order of the day for the World Champion. He retired in Canada, Detroit, France and Britain until a fifth place in Germany increased his points tally to five, but again in his home Grand Prix in Austria, he retired once more. By that time he'd had enough and on the Friday before the German Grand Prix he informed Ron Dennis that he was quitting the sport for good. He had won three World titles and no longer had the desire to continue. Dennis asked that he kept the news quiet so that he could find a replacement, but within a week had signed Rosberg (ironically bearing in mind the conversation that Keke and Niki had in Monaco) and so Lauda made the announcement public at his home Grand Prix. Sadly the press conference turned into an embarrassing affair as Ron Dennis, not Lauda's biggest fan at the best of times, used it to extol the virtues of his team and John Barnard in particular. Hardly any mention of Niki's achievements, although to his credit he did apologise to him immediately afterwards, but it was clear to the press pack that there was little love between the two. Sadly they continued to snipe and snarl at each other for the rest of the season and even if Lauda had wanted to stay for the next year, he probably wouldn't have been welcome. He did agree to see out this season though, and not walk away like last time.

He won the last of his twenty-five Grand Prix victories at the Dutch Grand Prix at Zandvoort, followed in second by Prost, although it was no traditional 'one-two' for the team as the Frenchman had harried and harassed Lauda throughout the race, but on this occasion the old campaigner was completely in command. He crossed the line just ahead of his team-mate and delighted in his quarter-century victory, but the delight didn't seem to transmit itself to his team. His side of the garage celebrated, but the side that wanted a World Championship for Prost, including Ron Dennis, seem to view it as an unnecessary victory. Lauda was now keen to leave as soon as possible.

The elation he felt soon disappeared at Monza where again he retired, and then at Spa for the Belgian Grand Prix he ploughed into a guard rail after accelerator problems and promptly dislocated his thumb. It meant he couldn't compete in the race and was forced to miss the European Grand Prix at Brands Hatch, the race that saw Nigel Mansell finally take victory, but far more importantly, Alain Prost become World Champion for the first time. Niki Lauda sat at home and watched proceedings on his television.

In fact, he should have been mentally preparing for the end of his career, watching old team mate John Watson driving his car in his absence, until he received a quite extraordinary offer from Brabham boss Bernie Ecclestone. Bernie had just lost the services of Nelson Piquet to Williams and had approached Lauda with a six million dollar deal to drive for him in 1986. It was an astonishing offer and one that needed some serious thinking, even if he would have appeared quite mercenary and possibly ended up divorced by his wife. As it was, Lauda thought it through and decided he no longer wanted the hassle of Formula One and he declined. It was probably due to the total lack of interest in his welfare from Ron Dennis, who by now had become a firm enemy in Lauda's mind, but whatever the reason, Lauda stuck by his decision to walk away.

The South Africa Grand Prix saw Lauda struggle in qualifying, not helped by Dennis's refusal to give him a spare car, but in the race he managed to get into the lead before the turbo engine expired in a now usual fashion for the outgoing World Champion.

His last race was on 3rd November 1985 at the season-ending Australian Grand Prix, and as Lauda readily admitted, he'd set his own personal record for the worst race preparation in his eighteen-year career after spending the previous evening drinking wine at a sponsors' party and chatting amiably to Ron Dennis all evening. Again he'd struggled in qualifying, putting the car sixteenth on the grid, yet in typical Lauda-fashion managed to conserve his tyres, when all others were shredding theirs, and took the lead with around thirty laps left. Sadly, motor racing doesn't do sentiment that well, and instead of leaving Formula One on the back of an emotional victory, he left it with the McLaren parked against a wall after the brakes had failed. In a way it matched exactly the scenario played out six years earlier with Hunt and Wolf at Monaco.

There were few goodbyes, although he had somehow rescued a modicum of a relationship with Ron Dennis and they wished each other well. In fact Niki was invited to an end-of-season party, but after saying farewell to his mechanics and a few well-meaning journalists, he caught a flight back to London almost immediately. Bernie Ecclestone was also on the flight and made one last attempt to lure him back by increasing his offer, but Lauda whose incredible resistance to financial temptation has to be admired and questioned in equal measure again declined politely. He was out of the sport and ready to embrace a new life. Not before wife Marlene – now metaphorically breathing a huge sigh of relief – threw a huge retirement party at their house in Ibiza. For him, and especially for her, that life was now over. Now time for another one.

CHAPTER TWENTY EIGHT

James and his 'dippers'

James Hunt had become a troubled man. After the initial honeymoon period following his retirement, he had soon lost interest in most of his passions and had started to look for some meaning in his life. Like many sportsmen and women who have retired from an active life, it can be difficult to replace the buzz that the initial one had generated. One man recently who has spoken eloquently about the problem was former England cricket captain Michael Vaughan, who admitted that he had suffered depression once his career had come to an end, and the British boxer Herol Graham had experienced even more extremes after his spotlight had faded. For James Hunt, it was a serious problem to contend with, yet only his close friends and Sarah were aware of his 'dippers' as he called them.

On the outside, Hunt looked like the James of old. The partying continued in the rambling mansion that was his Wimbledon home, and he continued his interest in golf and budgerigars, plus kept his hand in on the Formula One scene by co-commentating with the BBC alongside Murray Walker. They kept an unusual schedule around Grand Prix weekends. If it was a European race, quite often one or both of them would attend practice, but would be forced to return to the Television studios at TVC in London to commentate on the race itself, but if it was a 'long haul' race, then neither of them would see a car in anger close-up all weekend, only seeing what the viewer was seeing on a monitor in the darkened studio. Thankfully the viewer was blissfully una-ware in an age when those things really didn't matter too much to either the BBC or the people who watched it even when James railed against the apart-heid regime whilst covering the South African Grand Prix, and then calmy announced how pleased he was that he wasn't actually there. No-one noticed or complained.

Privately James was now a troubled man. The sense of responsibility didn't sit comfortably on his shoulders, even after Freddie was born in July 1987 at Mount Alvernia hospital in Guildford. Lord Hesketh was the godparent, continuing the link with the old days, and in the same autumn, James celebrated his 40th birthday with a huge party at their home. It was fancy dress and James cavorted around in just a kilt with little else, whilst Sarah dressed as a budgie, in honour to the theme of 'bird or beast'. By this time, James had rekindled his passion for breeding budgerigars and had built a large aviary where he kept around 150 birds, all worth a sizeable amount, which included blue and green Normals, Cinammons and Spangles – all breeds well known to experts. He took it all seriously and was soon showing them around the country, transported in an old 1957 A35 Austin van that he'd acqquired, and after a while the aviary was adorned with prize-winning rosettes and trophies. He also bought himself a Mercedes 6.9 litre saloon, but in later years that could be seen forlornly parked outside his home minus its wheels to avoid paying any car insurance or tax.

The budgerigars took over his life and there were times when he would leave Sarah alone with the children and spend hours in the aviary. Even if he was throwing a party, he would sometimes disappear and be found later sat amongst his birds watching as they flew around him making pleasant and soothing sounds. It seemed as if his life was calming, although there were still moments of mischief that kept him in the headlines.

One night, after a he'd won a prize with a top budgerigar, he decided to celebrate in town. He was in Doncaster in South Yorkshire, and after arriving at a night club slightly the worse for wear not only physically after drinking heavily, but his attire didn't match the requirements the doorman refused entry. There was a scuffle, hot coffee was thrown and Hunt was arrested by two policemen. The whole incident was recorded on CCTV, and for reasons only known to themselves, it was shown on a British TV station some years later as part of a documentary on James. There is something incredibly sad in watching a former Formula One World Champion being denied entry quite correctly too as the doorman was doing his job in the right manner to a nightclub and the subsequent scenes that could be seen in any town or city at night around the country when the perpetrator had consumed too much alcohol.

After a couple of hours in prison, he was released and all charges were dropped, but it was a contrite and apologetic James Hunt who sought out the doorman later to offer his explanations and remorse. The newspaper headlines again portrayed him in a poor light and it was clear that his life was unravelling at an alarming rate. His friend, Bubbles Horsley, believed that he had been born with 'a black dog on his shoulder', the kind of dark and depressing moods that used to haunt the British Prime Minister Winston Churchill, who referred to those times as the days of the 'black dog'. Horsley went on: 'I think that after the initial "honeymoon" of retirement from racing, the black dog came and sat on his shoulder and wouldn't go away'

He became uncommunicative and seemed to shy away from physical contact and at one stage even went to see a psychiatrist to analyse his inner feelings, but it seemed the best they could offer was that James was a 'bit of a cold fish'. His ex, Jane Birbeck, met him once and was shocked at what she saw. She said that he had fallen into despair and was wearing the dirtiest pair of jeans plus hadn't washed for some time. A mixture of alcohol and marijuana was helping in short measure, but hindering in the long term and his 'dippers' became longer and more pronounced. They would take over his life and he would then retire to his bed for days on end.

One such occasion was at Christmas, where he fell into such a deep depression that he spent all of Christmas in bed crying, even though Sarah and the boys were busy enjoying everything that the festive period offers a 'happy' family. She tried to help, but at time it must have been exasperating as she also had Tom and Freddie to look after too, even though the presence of Winston was a help. Eventually it became too much for Sarah too and she inevitably started drinking and losing weight. They saw marriage counsellors and more psychiatrists together, but if there was a lost cause at that time, it was James and nothing seemed to help his condition. There were financial clouds on the horizon too and in October 1988 Sarah and James separated.

At first they continued to live in the same house for the sake of the children, but when that was plainly unlikely to work, James bought a £350,000 house around the corner and moved Sarah, Tom and Freddie in and continued to visit. The marriage had crumbled, his relationship with his two sons was intermittent at best, the depression was deeper than ever and soon he would be on the verge of bankruptcy. It was the depths of time for James Hunt and the man who had delighted, appalled and amused the sporting nation at the same time was now falling into the abyss.

Within a year Sarah and James were divorced on the grounds of his adultery and sadly it was a messy and unpleasant affair. Sarah fought against her husband as she had felt the harmed party and the proceedings were expensive and bitter. There were suggestions that James would only be allowed to see his children when another adult was present, but thankfully common sense prevailed, but it was James who seemed to suffer the most.

Sarah had wanted a husband and children after her party years, and in James she felt she had found one, but James Hunt was incapable of commitment, something she found to her cost, and so quite rightly she fought for everything she could during the divorce. For James it meant his spiral into depression accelerated and his 'dippers' became more frequent with three-day binges on vodka, cigarettes and drugs. Add to that his financial situation deteriorated rapidly.

The divorce had cost a fortune, plus he became victim of being a Lloyd's Name and lost money with syndicates to the tune of around £200,000. He had put his name to a new £2 million James Hunt Racing Centre in Milton Keynes, but it closed almost immediately after it opened and it devoured yet more of his money. He felt unhappy with the way the divorce was handled by his solicitors and sued them, obtaining Legal Aid to fight the case all of which ate into his dwindling funds.

To help with his income, currently propped up in meagre fashion by the BBC commitments, he wrote a newspaper column that would be published in the *Independent, Daily Mail* and *Daily Telegraph*, something which he approached very seriously indeed. With the help of Gerald Donaldson, a respected journalist and later his biographer, he spent hours researching and gathering information to make his columns as interesting and accurate as possible.

Amazingly at the age of 41 he decided to give Formula One another go and arranged a private test session of a Williams car at the Paul Ricard circuit in France. It didn't work as he was around two seconds off the pace and the interest from the team was lukewarm. He approached his friend John Hogan, who had been so instrumental in his early racing days in arranging sponsorship and contracts, but Hogan could see it was the wrong move and told him so in a way only a close friend could. That avenue was closed, and after the divorce, which left him bitter and angry and as Sarah had said he had become victim of the 'the three Ls: Love, lawyers and Lloyd's', he found himself with little money to live on and a life drifting from one dark hole to the next.

CHAPTER TWENTY NINE

James reforms

Whatever it was that changed James Hunt's life, it could not have come a moment too soon. He had fallen into a black depression that only those who have experienced can truly understand the depths and the difficulty in fighting back. One of those was a friend called Mike Dennett, who had met James after his racing career had ended and had somehow become part of the circle of friends at the Wimbledon house. Dennett was a creative director in an advertising agency, and he too suffered from bouts of depression, and for that reason James invited him to move into the house. The presence of another must have helped James, especially someone who understood why he was drinking so heavily and why for days on end he would lay in bed and not talk to anyone.

The divorce had hit Hunt badly, both financially and emotionally. When he was threatened with not seeing his children, (the antics on the British Airways flight being cited as a good reason for him not being responsible enough to look after two small boys) it shocked him into action and he decided to fight back. He cut back on the drink and started to eat healthily. He tried all kinds of treatments to help cure himself, including herbal medicines and visited therapists, psychologists, psychiatrists and psychoanalysts. He took up cycling, as a way of keeping fit and of saving money, and slowly but surely be beat his addictions and started to think and act more clearly and rationally. By sheer force of will power and self-discipline, James Hunt came out of his 'black dog' days and his life started to improve. It was the kind of self-belief that he'd shown when first attempting motor racing on a shoestring budget, and the kind that took him to the World Championship against all of the odds in 1976, and it was the kind that was now going to embrace a new life for himself.

He started to attend Grands Prix again and his new enthusiasm for the sport was shown when he became an advisor to the Lotus team and helped with the drivers' race strategies, plus he also became a public relations ambassador for Shell Petroleum, who paid him for a sponsored version of his racing column. He was even welcomed in the Marlboro-McLaren motorhome by Ron Dennis, a man who apparently would never hire anyone with dirty fingernails, but he was more than happy to have James there in his usual attire of T-shirt and shorts with scruffy sandals. James had certainly changed his attitude to life, but convention was not part of his make-up and he would continue to dress exactly as he pleased for the rest of his life.

Suddenly he was the 'blue-eyed boy' of the paddock once more, and the journalists who had trembled with apprehension in the late 70s when forced to meet him, now found him a thoroughly charming and pleasant man. They even excused him turning up at a memorial service for the former World Champion Denny Hulme (the only driver from New Zealand to have won the title, but sadly later died of a heart attack) wearing his usual dress and cycling with a rucksack on his back. To be fair to James, he did actually get changed into a rumpled suit outside the church before venturing in.

One man who certainly noticed the change was Murray Walker and it hit him when they were having dinner before a Grand Prix and he'd asked James what he wanted to drink. James replied that he would take orange juice as he'd had his 'fair share' of alcohol. It was an amazing and truly impressive transformation for a man who was staring his demise straight in the eyes. As Walker said, there must have been many reasons such as the need to earn money, the need to look after his sons, his health was in serious danger and 'possibly more than anything else, he had a good woman behind him' That was now so true.

Niki Lauda enjoyed his retirement. Maybe 'enjoy' was not quite the right word, as his breakneck speed life was transferred from the race track to the skies as he concentrated on building up Lauda Air. Although founded in 1979, it started operations in 1985, the year that saw Lauda walk away from Formula One for the second and last time. Through hard work, long hours and the predictable Lauda will-to-succeed, he took on the huge state owned Austrian Airlines and managed to compete alongside them despite numerous attempts to close him and the airline down.

In 1987 scheduled operations were licensed and by 1990 an International flight licence was obtained. Lauda Air offered long-haul flights to Sydney and

Melbourne and it was clear that the company had a big future. Niki himself continued to run the airline, still wearing his Parmalat baseball hat to cover his wounds from the accident in 1976. He later admitted that the company paid him a fortune to continue to wear the cap whenever he was in public with their branding emblazoned across the front and he continued to face whatever problem face-on.

For him Formula One was in the past, and there was little acknowledgement of what was taking place in his absence. The cars were becoming faster and more lethal and the show was inevitably more spectacular. New names were appearing and the famous Prost-Senna battles were on the verge of taking centre stage. For Alain Prost, it must have felt slightly surreal as he had now taken the place of elder statesman at McLaren, whilst the young charger Senna stole the headlines, and in some ways the victories too, the position that Prost had filled some years previous to Lauda.

1991 was a traumatic year for Niki. On the 26th May one of his planes, a Boeing 767, crashed into the jungle near Bangkok in Thailand, killing all 223 people on board. It was discovered that after take-off from Bangkok, a stopover from Hong Kong to Vienna, a computer malfunctioned and the thrust reverser of the engine deployed. The pilots attempted to over-ride, but were unsuccessful, and 16 minutes after leaving the runway, debris was scattered all over the jungle along with the bodies of those inside. Niki personally visited the site and helped in the recovery process, and after an investigation, all Boeing 767s were recalled for modifications.

One can only imagine the feelings and emotions of Niki when confronted with the fact that one of his airliners had crashed and the people who flew with him had died. It must have been one of the most traumatic of times, and it was around this time that he and wife Marlene divorced. They had been together for 16 years, married for 15 and produced two sons, and during that time Marlene had been alongside Niki throughout his turbulent, dangerous and successful career. Now it was over. 1991 had not been kind to Niki Lauda.

CHAPTER THIRTY

Peace at last

Helen Dyson was a 25-year-old waitress working in a restaurant called 'Hamburger Heaven' in Wimbledon when she first met James Hunt. At first she hadn't noticed his attentions, as he looked like any other customer who would come in frequently, very frequently it seemed, smile, eat his food and then leave. What she was not aware of was that James Hunt was smitten by the girl 18 years his junior.

She was a blonde and beautiful, but her mind was set on her career as she was looking to become a successful artist and the waitressing was a way of earning money whilst she painted at night. She studied at Middlesex Poyltechnic, where she obtained a degree in fine arts and fabric design, and actually lived across the common from James with her parents Molly and Mark Dyson. She had few ideas who James was and certainly had no clue as to how famous he was. As she said later: 'If I had known who he was I might not have the courage to have said yes (when he asked her out). I thought he was some charming village man and that it was sweet of him'.

Their first date apparently was quite formal and stilted with conversation lacking somewhat, but she seemed to be impressed enough to see him again, and soon they became partners. Helen was a Catholic and when James told her of his past, she was genuinely shocked and questioned whether she wanted to have a relationship with someone who had found it impossible to be faithful. She was also concerned as to what her parents might think, but on their first meeting, they found him charming, and as the only concern she had expressed to them was about the age difference, their dismissal of such a thing meant that the security of the relationship was tightened. Even in the early days, Helen was not fully aware of how famous James was, only being slightly bemused when they went to restaurants and he was harried for autographs and pictures. Of course she would still have been at school when he was becoming Formula One World Champion, and in an age without the internet and twenty-four hour news coverage, it was difficult to find such information something which the twenty-first century citizen now takes for granted.

She also became a willing step-mother at an early age, taking control of Tom and Freddie when they came to spend the weekend, and it was something she clearly relished. For James it opened up his heart and feelings, especially to his two boys as he had felt he had let them down badly when he and Sarah had divorced and although he loved them, time spent with them was minimal and this was a guilt that stayed.

James Hunt, still financially embarrassed and struggling to make ends meet, was a much happier person after he met Helen. It could be said that she effectively saved his life at that time. The money was never a problem as far as he was concerned and as he said to his live-in friend Mike Dennett, 'I've been broke before', and he had friends aplenty who would help if needed. There are stories of Bernie Ecclestone loaning a significant amount and leaving it in a brown envelope for James to pick up at his office so as to pay some rather pressing bills, and old-friend and fellow racer Tony Dron repairing the sturdy Austin Van for free before an MOT. He hit the low as far as finances were concerned, but he was never in a poverty situation. There was always enough to get by, but the smoking and drinking and drug-taking were tempered depending on the cost. It was one way of beating an addiction.

Emotionally he was a happier person too. Although it is being a little presumptious to believe that in fact he was totally loyal to Helen, it was obvious that she had become the love-of-his-life and he would write long and passionate letters to her in his schoolboy-writing at races and then fax them immediately. He was also a lot better at refusing the advances of women at Grand Prix weekends as his heart now lay with Helen. He had even rebuilt his relationship with Sarah and they spoke often on the phone, eventually using his unique term of affection 'Beast' when they talked. He sent her all of the unpleasant letters they had exchanged during the messy divorce proceedings and asked her to burn them. As she said, they were still 'soul-mates'.

Helen finally moved into his home in 1992, although he had been trying to get her there for some time. Her independent nature and her desire to forge a career as an artist were the stumbling blocks, but he encouraged her to continue and even set up a studio above his snooker room and obtained commissions from private houses for her to paint. They had planned to buy another home, but she soon fell in love with the rambling house and they repainted the front and tidied it to make it more of a family home. There were no more parties, as Helen herself wasn't a party animal and when she said she was bored of watching the budgerigars when he was away at weekends, he simply sold them.

His new passion was for snooker and as well as the room he had built especially, he would often cycle to the RAC club in London and play for hours. It was a different James that lived in the early 1990s. Outside he looked the same. He bucked convention at every opportunity, wearing the scruffiest T-shirt and shorts with sandals and brown socks, and felt no hint of embarrassment of conscience when he would turn up at a formal occasion and get changed outside the front door in full view of passers-by. He still took the occasional drug, remembered by another good friend, Doctor Sid Watkins a neurosurgeon and the man in charge of the health and safety of Grand Prix drivers at race weekends, a man who had helped the sport become safer with his state-of-the-art medical facilities. There were few drivers that Watkins had grown close too (Ayrton Senna was one) but James was certainly part of that inner-circle and he and the boys would regularly travel up to Scotland for a weekend of relaxing and fishing on the Tweed. It was there where he would often smoke a 'joint' in the peace and tranquillity of his surroundings.

Inside he was a happy and contented man. The 'dippers' had gradually faded away, helped in no small way by Helen's presence and for the first time in his life he felt he was in love. It was a baffling phenomenon for him as he had always felt he was incapable of such a thing, something he put down to a lack of parental love when he was young beliefs that upset Sue his mother but he felt that at long last he was blossoming as a human being. After attending his parents' fiftieth wedding anniversary, Sue and Wallis expressed that they had never seen him so happy, taking his sons to the lake to feed the ducks and being a pleasant and charming man.

At home he doted on Helen. They lived the life of domestic bliss, still with Winston to wait on them and ate in the evenings in front of the television. He had become obsessively healthy and took a potion of ginger, lemon juice, honey and hot water every morning, plus ice-cold baths to strengthen his immune system. He had long foregone the usual cleansing procedures of soap and deodorant, believing that the body cleans itself naturally and he felt that it made him smell more like a man. He was happy. He was content. He had a loving partner, two wonderful children, he still worked alongside Murray Walker at the BBC meaning he could continue to be involved with the sport that made him, and he had a future. Sadly, it was not a fairy-tale happy-ending. Some people don't live happily-ever-after, and James and Helen were destined not to have the life they so desired.

CHAPTER THIRTY ONE

Farewell too early

If a fiction writer had penned the last few days of James Hunt's life, it couldn't have been as poignant or as emotional as the reality. By June 1993, he and Helen had decided to have children, and in the second week she had gone away on a final 'girls' holiday' with good friend Christina, who was also hoping to start a family with her boyfriend. It was the first time she had been away without James, but he had endorsed it and spent most of the previous night helping her to pack. The Greek island of Lesbos was the spectacular destination, and Helen went away without a care in the World.

James, who hated being alone, invited his occasional house-mate Mike Dennett to spend the weekend, and with Tom and Freddie due to be at the Wimbledon home too, it made for a hectic two or three days. On Friday nght, after putting the boys to bed and making them say their prayers, something James was very keen on, he and Mike then played snooker until the hours of the morning. Later on Saturday they watched the Rugby Union Test between the British Lions and the All-Blacks, and that evening with Winston baby-sitting the two boys, he and Mike attended a small and quiet party thrown by old friends Chris and Suzy Jones. There was no suggestion of the tragedy to come.

On Sunday the day of the Canadian Grand Prix James cycled the six miles to BBC Television Centre, parked his bike outside the front entrance and got changed before meeting Murray Walker in the studio to do their live commentary. This was another 'long haul' race that they weren't attending, but commentating on from the live 'feed' from the Canadian broadcasters. With the help of producer Mark Wilkin – a long and trusted friend of James who down the years had indulged his antics due to his incredible talent and passion behind the microphone, and because he genuinely liked him – the broadcast went off without a hitch. For the record, although it is a mere passing note to the story, Alain Prost won the race in the Williams.

James said goodbye and arranged to meet Wilkin the following Tuesday as he had already confided in him a detail of a personal nature concerning his intentions for Helen. Wilkin was pleased and they confirmed lunch. Saying farewell to Walker, James cycled home and was just in time to see Tom and Freddie being collected by Sarah.

James and Sarah now got on famously and the two sat and talked over coffee, before she departed with the boys. Then Mike Dennett sat down with James to watch highlights of the Grand Prix, which James always appreciated so that his analysis could be praised or criticised in equal measure. This was a James Hunt who could now take personal and professional comments in the way they were meant. He had grown up, and as he had confided in Wilkin, he felt his life was starting again.

On Monday James wrote his newspaper column, agonised over it and had it checked and re-checked before submission, and then telephoned Helen at her hotel in Greece. What follows is certainly the poignancy of love and commitment, but nevertheless it is true. Although they had discussed marriage in the past, and it certainly wasn't the spur-of-the-moment, the fact is that during the phone-call James officially asked Helen to marry him. She was overjoyed and as she later said to Gerald Donaldson: 'He proposed to me and I accepted', and then with unbelievable sadness she added: 'It was the last time I ever spoke to him'.

She put the phone down with one assumes a feeling of total ecstacy, whilst James was reported by Mike Dennett as being much lighter of heart and full of spirit. The two played a marathon snooker match, only interrupting it for a spaghetti meal. It was only then that James stated to feel 'really shitty' as he described it and so took a break from the match. He was sufficiently concerned to call a friend who knew a little about medical matters, but as he was speaking the pain and the numbness that had travelled over his body and arms receeded, so he took no further notice.

With the huge benefit of hindsight and also not being present, it is easy now to say that the first thing he and Mike should have done was to call an ambulance and get quickly to hospital, but James Hunt was a strong-willed and forceful man who had lived a life that others could only dream of or fear. He had overcome the danger of a motor racing circuit time and again and had retired at the right time so as to prolong his life. He had also beaten the demons of drink and drugs and was now healthier and happier. Who would argue against such a position?

What is known is that Mike retired to bed after midnight and heard James pottering around downstairs in the kitchen making his end-of-night coffee. He then fell asleep.

The next morning, after rising at around ten and seeing no sign of James, he went to his room. He was on the floor in his dressing-gown, with his two dogs next to him. James Hunt was dead. A massive heart attack had killed him as he'd attempted to climb the stairs to his bedroom and in no time at all an ambulance had been called and his body was taken away. At the age of just 45, the man who had calculated that he could reasonably expect to further his life expectancy to around 75 once he walked away from the most dangerous sport in the world, had died. His body finally crying out 'enough' following the years of abuse and hard-living. Ironic that he was now as clean living as he had ever been.

James Hunt, 1976 Formula One World Champion, father of two young boys and future husband of name-only fiancée, Helen, had died. The baby who had arrived into the world kicking and screaming, had left with barely a whimper. The man who had epitomised what a 'racing driver' really should be like, the archetypal playboy who lived fast on the circuit and off it, and who had shown the same type of free spirit seen in the likes of Mike Hawthorn and Innes Ireland, was no more. Now his nearest and dearest, including Helen, and then the world-at-large would need to know.

Poor Mike Dennett had the terrible task of informing everyone of the death. James' brother Peter came to the house to take charge of proceedings and deal with the press, who very quickly arrived outside. His parents were devastated as could be expected, as was the whole family. Sarah could not quite believe it and had to break the news to Tom and Freddie, who had only been with their father a day or so earlier. She took tremendous courage in the response of Tom, who after all of the tears, told her that: 'His spirit will always be with us' as James had taught his sons to believe in God strongly and that God was everywhere and everyone is a spirit of God.

Niki Lauda was 'just devastated by the news of his death. From my point of view James was an incredible personality because you could see him with people on the street, talking low-key, maybe, and you could even put him at the table with the Queen of England. For me he was the most charismatic personality who's ever been in Formula One'

Friends from his racing and broadcasting days were stunned. Tony Dron cried, Lord Hesketh was 'absolutely shattered', Bubbles Horsley regarded James as his best friend and took it very badly, and Murray Walker was left in shock. As he recounted to the author, his wife Elizabeth had approached him and asked him to sit down as there was a shock, and he immediately thought it was his dear 95-year-old mother, but when he heard it was James, rationale left completely and he said 'but I was only with him on Sunday as if that should stop him from dying'.

Of course Helen was the one who immediately suffered the most. It had taken some time to track her down in Greece and eventually after returning from a day-trip, she was told that there had been numerous phone calls from London. On hearing the news, she broke down in hysterics and only the presence of her friend, the kindness of the hotel staff and an extraordinarily generous gesture from McLaren boss Ron Dennis, who put his private jet at her disposal, helped her get through the day. When she arrived at the Wimbledon home, she fell into Peter's arms and for a while fell to pieces.

The funeral, six days later at St Mary's Church in Wimbledon, was attended by just family and close friends, around 30 in total. Wallis, bereft of his son, tried to make the proceedings a little more cheerful, saying James would have wanted it that way and afterwards they toasted him with a bottle of 1922 claret, something James had bought him for his 60th birthday. Sarah and the boys had placed a bouquet and their christening blanket on the coffin, whilst Helen had put the lead of his beloved dog Oscar inside. They all said goodbye quietly and privately to the man they had loved and still loved.

As the weeks passed, it became clear as to how well regarded James had become within the motor-sport world as journalists, who had one point almost loathed the man, had grown to like and admire him. There was a memorial service on the 29th September 1993 at St James's Church in Piccadilly where over 600 people attended, and speaker after speaker Stirling Moss, Innes Ireland, Murray Walker, Lord Hesketh and even Nigel Davison, an old teacher from Wellington College stood and shared their precious memories of him. Murray Walker had this to say:

'We're here today to remember and to honour James as a very special person, who in different ways has been a part of the life of each and every one of us. To his family, he was a loving son, brother, father. To the motor racing world of which he was such an outstanding part, he was a great competitor, a forceful teammate, a determined and gifted rival. And to millions of Formula One fans all over the world, from Adelaide to Andover, who listened to the calm, authoritative and witty television commentaries he gave, his was the voice that made sense out of an involved and complicated sport. And to me, he was a respected and admired colleague, whose wit and wisdom added immeasurably to our joint efforts to communicate the sport that meant so much to both of us.

But to everyone, James was a charismatic personality whose untimely departure has made our world a duller place. In today's world, most of us stand out like grey against black. Conforming to the general standard, unable or unwilling to do their own thing, make their own mark, be their own man. Which is something that you most certainly could not say about James.

Quite apart from his talents, his success, his commanding presence and his natural dignity, he was an immensely likeable, warm, different kind of human being. One who made wherever he was a livelier and more stimulating and enjoyable place to be. Because James didn't think like other people. He refused to conform to the rules that govern most of us. And he had the presence and the charm to get away with it.

I bet almost everybody here could tell a personal story about something that James did or said. And they'd tell it with affection and warmth, to emphasise that he was no ordinary person.

The first commentary I ever did with him was on a Formula 5000 race at Silverstone. When James, with his leg in plaster, lay on the floor, looking up at the monitor, at an extremely boring and uneventful race. When I handed him the microphone to sum it up, he simply said "What a load of rubbish!", and handed it back to me.

But later at Monaco, for his very first Grand Prix commentary wearing no shoes, a T-shirt, shorts that had certainly seen better days and clutching a bottle of rose, he planted his plaster cast in my lap and sailed into the comments that were to endear him to his vast following for 13 years.

Now our gathering here is to celebrate James's life rather than mourn his death much as we all do so. And I'm jolly sure that's what he'd like. You don't need me to tell you about his twin careers. About his Boy's Own Paper leap from virtual obscurity to World Champion in an incredibly short time. About how he became the nation's sporting hero and the focal point of their obsessive interest which was something he hated, incidentally. About how he retired from Grand Prix racing far too soon, dispirited by his lack of success in an uncompetitive car, when there isn't a shadow of a doubt that his talent could have made him World Champion again, and again. About how he effortlessly changed gear into a new role, as the BBC's voice of authority in Formula One.

James raced in an era where it was possible both to succeed and enjoy yourself. And he did both to the full. And then he matured, to pass on his experience and his knowledge to his successors, and an enormous audience, by means of that commanding voice, presence and his natural authority.

His sudden death, totally unexpected, and tragic for one so young and seemingly so fit, touched the nation like few things in my experience. It's a theory of mine that television communicates people to the viewer like they really are. And it certainly did in James's case. I have had dozens and dozens of truly moving letters telling me that the writers felt they'd lost a real and valued personal friend, whose warmth and humour had enriched their lives, and whose experience, knowledge and outspokenness had kindled and developed their interest in Grand Prix racing.

Now if my theory is correct, it's not difficult to see why. They saw James as a character, which he certainly was. They saw him as his own man, which he most certainly was. They saw him as having a bright, breezy, lively personality, which he did. And they loved his irreverence and his provocative comments. Because James, anywhere and everywhere, was never reluctant to speak his mind. An incredibly clear-thinking and analytical mind, which may sometimes have produced words his targets didn't like I didn't like some of them but which he was always ready to defend to their faces with logic and eloquence that usually won them over.

"I'm just off to have it out with so-and-so about last week", he'd say. And then you'd see him calmly justify his case in the paddock, when most people would have laid low and hoped that it would go away. But then he would always

apologise if he felt he'd been wrong. Apropos of which, I have never known a public figure of his magnitude, of his very considerable magnitude, who was as unaffected by his success and as self-effacing as James was.

Letter after letter told me how the writer had met him somewhere and been overwhelmed by the fact that he found the time to stop and just chat like any other enthusiast. You know, the paying public on the other side of the track get next-to-no direct contact with their heroes these days. But they got the consideration they deserved from James.

"One of the reasons I retired, Murray" he told me, "was that I just couldn't stand being a human honey pot wherever I went. Restaurants, pubs, out on the street. Everyone wanted a part of me. No privacy. No way I could lead a normal life". Hardly surprising when practically everything he did created national head-lines at the height of his racing fame. But James was essentially a private man, and he didn't really like the ceaseless adulation.

When his racing career was over, he was glad to get away from it, go about his new life forever accompanied by his beloved Oscar become a truly loving father, and do something which must have been totally out of character to most people: successfully breed and show budgerigars.

So a paragon of humanity? Nothing to criticise? No weak points? Well of course there were, and thank heavens too. None of us is perfect. There are people here who could write a book about James Hunt's escapades. And an immensely read-able best-seller it would be too. And when the adrenaline was running high, he could be a fearsome chap. I've seen him fell a rival competitor who angered him. I've seen him do the same to a marshal who incurred his wrath. I bet Teddy Mayer hasn't forgotten the roasting he got at the end of the Japanese Grand Prix whilst he was vainly trying to tell a furious James, who thought he'd failed, that he had in fact clinched the World Championship. And I certainly won't forget the tongue lashing that an unfortunate technician got in Australia when a communication failure made James look silly.

But, that same adrenaline surge gave him the selfless courage to rescue Ronnie Peterson from his blazing Lotus at Monza. Bravery can take many forms, but surely none greater than voluntarily plunging into fire to save your fellow man.

James could charm the birds out of the trees, but sadly he wasn't spared hard times in recent years. Personal and financial problems had made things very *tough for him. But you would never had known it. He was unfailingly cheerful and remained the kind, courteous and helpful English gentleman he had always been. And he industriously knuckled down to getting out of the trouble he was in.*

In his job as racing consultant, he passed on his hard-won knowledge and expertise to a new generation of drivers. Ask his friend and mentor, John Hogan. Ask Johnny Herbert. Ask Mika Hakkinen.

In his job as a TV commentator, he was a friend and talented contributor to his colleagues. Ask Jonathan Martin, the BBC's head of sport. Ask Mark Wilkin, the producer of Grand Prix. Ask me.

And in his new job as a journalist, he was a very welcome and lively addition to the press room. One who had shown the same dedicated determination to succeed as he had at the last three Grands Prix of 1976, where quite outstanding drives against the odds won him his World Championship.

On Sunday, 13th June, James cycled from his home in Wimbledon to the television centre at Shepherd's Bush, gave his customary, authoritative commentary on the Canadian Grand Prix, did his column and cycled home again, seemingly his usual self. Little more than 24 hours later, to stunned disbelief, he was no longer with us. Even now, it seems hardly conceivable that we're no longer going to enjoy his ebullient presence and it hasn't, somehow, all been a ghastly dream.

They say the gods take those they love early. In which case, we can only console ourselves with the knowledge that 45 years of James's life contained at least as much as 90 of anybody else's.

His loved ones, motor racing, his countless friends and all those who admired him from afar are infinitely the poorer for his passing. May he rest in peace.'

As well as the obvious sadness that accompanied the demise of James and affected his nearest and dearest, there are two stories that can almost be lost in the grief and despair, yet they show the immediacy that death can bring. On the morning of James dying, BBC producer and good friend Mark Wilkin called his home to confirm their lunch date. It was his brother Peter who answered the phone and told him the terrible news, and Nigel Roebuck, the then Autosport journalist and close friend, was at home about to write his obituary for the following week's edition. He had just returned from Canada and had not listened to his recorded telephone messages that had built-up in his absence. After listening to most, one of the last was the most poignant.

'Nigel, J. Hunt speaking. Six twenty-five Monday evening. Just calling for a gossip. If you're back tonight, give me a shout failing that, tomorrow perhaps'. It left Nigel 'trembling' and later the realisation that he, Mike Dennett and Helen were the last three people James Hunt spoke to before a few hours later collapsing and dying.

When the contents of James Hunt's Will were made public, and seized upon eagerly by the British tabloids, it was not pleasant reading. His total assets were around £1.2 million, but around £850,000 was owed to the banks and the remainder was put in a trust for his two sons. Sadly there was a lengthy disagreement between Sarah and Peter Hunt over the disbursement of the assets, but that thankfully was settled out of court. Also poor Helen found herself effectively homeless after the death of James, and she left the house with just a few personal momentos to cherish, as virtually everything else had been put away as either an asset or future investment for the two boys. She soon moved back into her parents' home, but eventually Peter came through with his promise of funds owed to her and she was able to set herself up in a small apartment and start life again. It must have been an almost impossible task, but according to Gerald Donaldson's biography of James, she faced it with fortitude and grace, telling herself that nothing in her life could ever be as bad again. She, amongst all of the grieving mourners, was the one who seemed to have had the cruellest time as she never lived the life that they had planned.

For Niki Lauda, who had seen so many of his colleagues and friends die, usually on the track, the death of James Hunt didn't make a lot of sense. Lauda had beaten the odds in 1976 and had walked away twice from the sport with limbs and faculties intact, despite the scarring on his face and the possible mental scarring that had impacted too, yet James Hunt, a man who was as brave and talented as he on the track and lived life beyond the full off it, had died of something as almost mundane as a heart attack. He would miss his friend.

CHAPTER THIRTY TWO

Another return for Niki

1991 had been a bad year for Niki Lauda. His airline had suffered a tragedy with the crash that had killed so many people, and as well as the human toll, there was inevitably a financial effect too. In the world of business, it is something that is never far from the story and it is possible that Lauda Air suffered due to the horrendous crash in the jungle. As well as the obvious emotional strain that had been put on Niki, his marriage to Marlene had failed and they had divorced, yet as with all of the strands of the Lauda story, there was always a positive side. He was back in Formula One.

Ferrari, as matches their volatile Italian temperament, had again gone from world-beaters to mid-grid strugglers in the space of around twelve months. They had struggled for a few years until Alain Prost breathed new life into the team in 1990 but he was the sacked for making negative comments about the car and by 1991 they were in such disarray that the old tried and trusted method of dismissing everyone and re-arranging the team by putting square blocks in round holes was clearly not working. Another drastic measure was needed and like 18 years previously, they turned once more to Luca di Montezemolo to sort out the mess. He was actually made Director of the team and was given a free hand to do whatever he wanted and one of the first things he did was to turn to his old friend Niki Lauda to help.

'Old Man' Ferrari had died a few years previously, actually on the 14th August 1988, leaving a team now trying to find its new identity, and for Lauda, any feelings of betrayal or anger he may have felt thirteen years ago, had now evaporated and he returned to a team that he had genuine affection for. His role was as an overseer on the pit wall and a guiding hand for the two Italians who were driving for this most Italian team Jean Alesi and Ivan Capelli. Enzo Ferrari had hardly ever employed an Italian driver whilst he ran his team with an iron hand, and it was something that had always angered the Italian tifosi. Now they had two capable and at times fast Italians in the scarlet cars, but not regular race-winners. It was down to Lauda to try and change that.

The car for 1992 was a disaster and no amount of coaxing and advice could alter that fact. By the end of the season the team made the most un-Ferrari like decision by employing John Barnard, the former technical-director at McLaren to shape things in an English-type way. The problem was that he was happy to continue to work in England, so the team became fractured, and even the brilliant Barnard's physical presence in Maranello failed to turn the fortunes around. Within a year there was another change with the arrival of the focused and ambitious Jean Todt. The Frenchman had masterminded Peugeot's success in the World Rally Championship and had come to the 'Prancing Horse' with one remit. Make Ferrari winners again!

He of course did what all good and ambitious new managers do well. He cleared out the old staff and replaced them with new, and that included Niki Lauda. Todt was unconvinced that the Austrian had been successful in his role and so with ruthless lack of sentiment, Lauda was released from his duties. He didn't go without first spending an inordinate amount of time persuading a brilliant driver by the name of Michael Schumacher to join the team. The then two-times World Champion joined in 1996, but by then Lauda had gone. Todt, Schumacher and a brilliant technician called Ross Brawn then created history as they literally re-wrote the history books as Ferrari dominated the World Championship for years, giving Schumacher five more titles and more victories then any other driver.

1994 of course saw the tragic events of the San Marino Grand Prix, from the 29th April to the 1st May, where Roland Ratzenberger and then the great Ayrton Senna were killed, plus Rubens Barichello was seriously injured in another separate incident. Niki Lauda, still a regular attendee of Grand Prix events, then spent some time revitalising the old Grand Prix Drivers Association which had effectively disbanded since his retirement. It gave the drivers a greater say on safety once more just like the days of Jackie Stewart and Formula One was again in the spotlight for the wrong reasons. The sport had been rudely shaken by the events in Imola and in a way it was another of those defining moments as yet more stringent safety measures were introduced. Most people believed that if a talent the like of Senna could be killed racing then it could conceivably happen to any of them. It needed the calm and analytical mind of Niki Lauda to steer the new GPDA through its second re-birth.

To prove how the sport had still got a hold on Lauda, he agreed to join German TV station RTL as a pundit, very much in the James Hunt role that he had taken on at the BBC. This was despite the continuing pressure that running Lauda Air was exerting. It looked as if attending every race as an observer was something that was a relaxation and no longer a duty.

By the time of the end-of-the-century, Lauda Air was a big player, but was constantly battling the huge Austrian Airlines. Niki Lauda had successfully rebuffed their overtures time and again, but by 1999 fuel costs had spiralled and with the weakness of European currencies against the Dollar, Lauda Air found itself in trouble. Then after twenty years of fighting, Austrian Airlines finally seized 36% share in the company and effectively gained control. Niki was offered the post of Manager to the company that he had founded and built-up, and somehow he fulfilled that role until November 2000 he fell out with the board of directors and immediately resigned, although the whispers were that he was in fact sacked. As ever he was sanguine and relaxed about what had taken place.

"I built Lauda Air from nothing against a state monopoly to 22 aeroplanes. They wanted to run it their way, which can't work, so I left which is logical if things happen that you can't control...but I'd done it long enough". Niki Lauda was now looking for another challenge.

CHAPTER THIRTY THREE

The Jaguar debacle

Jackie Stewart is a man who in his career epitomised everything that was good and professional about the sport of motor racing. A three-times Formula One World Champion, a frighteningly fast and talented racing driver (who incidentally could also have won Olympic Gold at shooting had he continued to pursue that sport), a vigorous campaigner for safety improvements that undoubtedly saved the lives of many of his colleagues down the years, blessed with film-star looks and the first racing driver who really embraced sponsorship and the lifestyle that it could bring. He was a pace-setter in every sense of the description.

With that in mind, it was hardly surprising that the team that he eventually took into Formula One at the end of the 90s with his son Paul – Ford Stewart Racing – would be highly regarded in the paddock. This small team, which had already had success in the lower Formula series, racing against the powerhouses of Ferrari, McLaren, Benetton and Williams actually stood up and gave them a bloody nose by winning the 1998 European Grand Prix at the Nurburgring with Johnny Herbert at the wheel. It was a remarkable transformation of success from behind the wheel to success behind the pit wall for the likeable Scot, something which is a lot harder than it sounds (ask Alain Prost as to how difficult following the collapse of his uncompetitive Prost team that nearly broke him financially and presumably emotionally too). Stewart Racing could not hope to compete on an equal footing though without a huge cash injection, and so in 1999 the team was bought out by Ford, who immediately re-branded them Jaguar and be-decked the cars in the old British Racing green colours. They were to be the new patriotic British team, taking over the mantle from Hesketh, Lotus and Williams who had all tapped into the heart of the motor-sporting nation at some time. Also if Ford could embrace a bit of Jaguar history and create a bit of their own too, then it should be seen as an unqualified success. Sadly it was an unmitigated disaster.

2000 was a fiasco. The cars were middle-of-grid at best and the team struggled to live up to the fanfare that had heralded their arrival. Managing-Director and Ford Vice-President Wolfgang Reitzle acted swiftly and appointed Bobby Rahal to run the team, an appointment greeted with a certain amount of surprise by observers in the Formula One paddock. Rahal was a great and successful name in IndyCar racing in America, both as a driver and then team owner, but his experience of F1 was limited. He came with enthusiasm, but with little extra success as the team went from mid-grid to strugglers. At the beginning of 2001 Reitzle acted decisively. He wanted someone who knew the sport, had been successful and was a leader. Niki Lauda was still active around the F1 paddock, was still commentating for German television and now didn't have the extra pressure and burden of running his own airline. He was the obvious choice, and so now Lauda became Director of Premier Performance at Jaguar Racing.

It was a grand title and Lauda took to it with abandon, although his golden touch was missing when it came to the cars. Drivers Eddie Irvine and Pedro de la Rosa struggled and the team finished a lowly eighth out of eleven in the constructors' championship, not quite what Ford expected for their heavy investment. Soon it became clear that two leaders could not share the top spot and tensions grew between Rahal and Lauda (something which virtually everyone expected once Niki had been appointed with the exception of the man who made the appointment Reitzle). After Lauda learned that Rahal was in the process of selling Irvine to rival team Jordan, he pounced and in August 2001 fired him. The decision was taken with the full backing of the Ford management and it also meant that the role of Jaguar Team Manager was now Niki Lauda's. Lauda was infuriated over the Irvine situation, as Irvine had been one of James Hunt's protégés and he'd felt particularly close to the Irishman. In turn, Rahal was less than impressed with Niki's decision to allow another team to use the Ford V10 engine that was powering Jaguar. As it was, Rahal left within a year of joining. It was an unpleasant episode and one could feel sympathy for the American, but Lauda put it in his usual succinct way:

'Bobby Rahal had a lot of other jobs he was doing, flying backwards and forwards to the United States. A Formula One team doesn't work like this: Frank Williams and all those guys, they're there twelve hours a day, and that's what it takes if you want to beat them. I never wanted to take this job, but if you're in charge of the whole group and suddenly someone's missing in the most important part of it, the logic is to do it yourself'

Lauda took on full responsibility for the team and hired his former McLaren race engineer Steve Nicholls to help with the new Jaguar R3 car, which was launched with high hopes for the new season. To prove its worth, Niki actually drove it in a test session at the Valencia circuit, something which presumably didn't go down too well with regular drivers, Irvine and de la Rosa, and managed to spin twice in three laps, much to the amusement of the Irishman. As Lauda said tongue-in-cheek: 'I was told that I approached the corners as fast as de la Rosa. Unfortunately I didn't come out of them'. Even if he'd contemplated a return to the track, that episode would almost certainly persuade him otherwise.

The car was ready for the new season, and failed spectacularly. Lauda acted and immediately sacked Nicholls and appointed Gunther Steiner instead. It seemed a knee-jerk reaction, but slowly results started to pick up, culminating with a fighting third place for Irvine at the Italian Grand Prix, and then on 26th November 2002, Lauda himself was dismissed.

Ford were unhappy with the lack of results, and the new Vice President of the company, Richard Parry-Jones, was less than impressed with Lauda's input and replaced him with Tony Purnell, arguing that he had more technological knowledge than Niki Lauda. It was to be expected. When Niki had taken on the job as team manager, he had obviously taken on the burden of both success and failure, and frankly the Jaguar Formula One team was a catastrophic failure. At the age of 53 though, the Austrian was out of a job again.

The story of Jaguar continued with their downhill slide unstoppable. Ford were quite understandably unhappy with their car struggling at the back of the field, and also the fact that hardly any of their branding could be seen on the British racing green, and really could not see what they were getting for their money. Unsurprisingly soon afterwards they pulled the plug completely. They sold the team to the drinks manufacturers Red Bull and as the old cliché says, the rest is history. Red Bull went on to become one of the most successful Formula One teams in modern history and joined Ferrari and McLaren as the 'powerhouses' of the sport, taking driver Sebastian Vettel to four consecutive World Championships, with the promise of more to come. For the great name of Jaguar, the brief excursion into the cut-throat world of F1 was a poor reflection on a great sporting marquee and did not add any lustre to the history of the company, no matter what form that takes today.

Niki Lauda didn't sit around in early retirement after he had been sacked by Ford. A year later he embarked on a new challenge by acquiring the former Aero Lloyd Austria operation and set up flyNiki, a low cost airline. He then joined forces with Air Berlin and built up the company so that today it has around 650 employees. He also continued to sit at the cockpit and fly some of his planes himself, something which must have been quite a surprise to any unsuspecting passenger. Having a former Formula One World Champion fly you to your holiday destination is certainly worth remembering. In 2011 Niki sold the airline and presumably came out on top financially and with his head held high.

He continued to commentate for RTL on all Grands Prix, but was severely censured in 2010 when he described Robert Kubica as a 'polack' live on air during the Monaco Grand Prix, seemingly more a cheeky nickname as opposed to any hint of insult, but it was still a regrettable moment – and as far as his personal life was concerned, in 2008 he married Birgit, a former flight attendant for his airline who was 30 years his junior. In September 2009 she gave birth to twins, a boy and a girl called Max and Mia (he also has an illegitimate son Christoph) and also had a kidney donated to him after the one he had received from his brother years earlier failed. That was a situation that was hardly ever mentioned at the time, and he certainly didn't allow it to hinder his life, preferring to have the transplant and continue his life without any thought of recuperation or a slowing down.

When he was asked about being a father again at the age of 60, his response was typical Lauda: 'What does a young turk know of burping and changing nappies? I can do that and at night as well. I am fit and I am not senile yet. I am ecstatically happy'.

Niki Lauda is seen at the Grand Prix races regularly and has now taken on a role with the Mercedes F1 team, and with the recent revival of interest in the 1976 season in particular (a film called 'Rush' directed by Ron Howard is re-telling the story for the big screen), he is always in demand. An elder statesman of the sport, the three-times World Champion is now spoken of in the same breath as Alain Prost, Nelson Piquet Sr, Jackie Stewart and Graham Hill, yet few put him alongside the likes of Ayrton Senna or Juan-Manuel Fangio or even Michael Schumacher, who may not have been one of the 'greats' but set so many records with his seven World titles and near-one hundred Grand Prix victories. In fact it is unlikely that Lauda or Hunt for that matter would make too many 'top ten' lists, but their contribution to the sport has been immense.

Elder statesmen Lauda at the 2012 Texan Grand Prix

CHAPTER THIRTY FOUR

The Characters

Every life lived shares itself with a list of characters that play a small or a large part in their story. They help to shape, define and confirm their time, and they too should have the recognition of remembrance. For James Hunt and Niki Lauda, those characters helped shape their lives and played an enormous role in their story. Some have left us, most are still alive and I hope I have been accurate in describing where they have moved on to and what they are achieving with their lives now.

For James Hunt, his two sons, whom he doted on so much, will continue to carry their father's legacy. Brought up by mother Sarah after his death, they each trod a different path. For Tom, he was the academic and predictably attended Wellington College and then University, whilst Freddie seemed to take on the mantle of his father and the wayward ways that accompanied him. With his dad's personality and looks (the stooping gait and unkempt hair), he enjoyed his mother's passions for horses and polo, but after attending a Goodwood Festival of Speed event, he fell in love with motor racing and decided to make a full-time career out of it. He made his race debut on 29th October 2006 and actually managed to finish in an overall fourth place. Unfortunately (or fortunately as far as his mother was concerned) he realised he wasn't that good and retired early his last race was at the end of 2009 – but not before he'd had his father's name tattooed on his back.

The Hunt family continued after James's death and Peter in particular was instrumental in dealing with the financial affairs concerning the Hunt estate. It was he who had to take care of Helen and eventually agreed a settlement that meant she was looked after financially in the months following the death of his brother, but he also had the unpleasant task of gradually moving her out of the Wimbledon house she had shared with him, as it was in the process of being sold. In later years he contracted and beat cancer, showing the same kind of fortitude and resilience as his late brother.

David Hunt attempted to become a racing-driver too, this despite the fact that James had told him that he had no intention of helping him financially, or indeed in any other way, as he didn't want to be responsible should something terrible happen to him. He raced in the lower formulae with limited success, competing in Formula Ford and Formula Three from 1983 to 1987, and then progressed to Formula 3000 and actually had a test session with the Benetton Formula One team before giving up.

He was in the news recently after he sold the rights to the Team Lotus name when it returned to F1 racing. He'd actually bought the team in 1994 when it collapsed, but had done little with it, until Formula One decided that they were looking for new teams to join the series in an age of cost-cutting and openness. Lotus was one of the teams allowed to enter under franchise, but the one owned by Malaysian Tony Fernadez bore no relation to that run so unbelievably successfully by Colin Chapman and resurrected by David. In fact David had sold his team and the name to the Litespeed Formula Three outfit and they later applied to enter F1 in 2010, but were refused entry. After struggling at the back of the grid for two years, 'Team Lotus' lost a court case to retain the name (which subsequently went to the Renault team) and re-named itself Caterham. It is fair to say that Formula One is low on sentiment.

Of the other brothers and sisters, Tim became a big name in the art world, after temporarily being a male model, something his late brother would surely have approved of, and is now a Director of the Andy Warhol foundation in New York. Sally and Georgina made their way in life in a caring capacity as a lay pastoral assistant and a charity worker respectively.

Sue lost her husband Wallis in 2001 after a long battle with illness and a memorial service was held at Wellington College, a place so intrinsically linked to the Hunt household.

James of course had many partners in his life. In fact if it were possible to list them all then any book would be doubled in size, but there are a handful who were special to him down the years and these are the ones who have been mentioned in this book.

Taormina Rich, or 'Ping' as she was called, actually married Peter Rieck shortly after she split with James after meeting him at the 1970 Monaco

Grand Prix. At the time she was still dating James. The three actually became great friends and now 'Ping' and her husband live in Cambridgeshire.

Jane 'Hottie' Birbeck actually had a relationship with the athlete Daley Thompson after she split with James and they were together for around twelve years. She never married, and according to a recent biography of James Hunt, she has never spoken to anyone outside of Gerald Donaldson about her time with James. She apparently lives a quiet life and prefers it that way.

Sarah was the one who went through the most traumatic time following her ex-husband's death. Faced with the task of bringing up two young boys alone, without the obvious male influence a father can bring, she candidly admits that she struggled. She ended up in a huge battle with the Hunt family over the estate and what was owed to her sons, which thankfully was eventually resolved amicably. She though went into a mental spiral, suffering panic attacks, and only after taking on part-time jobs as a waitress or barmaid did she regain her self-esteem and self-belief. As she said when talking about the possibility of getting married again: 'I didn't believe it would ever happen again. I was one hundred per cent certain that the right man could not be found'.

The right man did come along though in the shape of Lieutenant Colonel Christopher Jeffery of the Royal Gurkha Regiment. They met in 1977 and she actually proposed to him within a month of their meeting! They lived in Nepal, where his regiment was based, whilst Tom and Freddie were at boarding school, and after being transferred to Germany, they had a son together Charlie. Sadly, this was another story not to have the happy-ever-after fairytale ending. When Charlie was just seven months old, dad Christopher had a stroke whilst watching the 1999 Japanese Grand Prix on the television. Two days later, at the age of 52, he died. Sarah was effectively widowed for the second time in her life. The army took care of her financially and she bought a rambling country house in Hampshire, where she continued to bring up her three sons.

Helen of course was left completely alone. The life they had planned never took place, and after the funeral she struggled to come to terms with his death. Sadly she was forced to leave the house they had shared for the last twelve months or so, and she moved back in with her parents. Even sadder was the fact that she wasn't able to take any of the possessions as Sarah had itemised them all as a keepsake for the boys' future. She also didn't see much of Tom and Freddie afterwards either, something which must have upset her, as she had played a part in their upbringing when they had come to stay.

Emotionally, Helen said that she came out of the despair once she had bought her own apartment and started anew. It was a place that held no memories of her time with James and she even described it as a 'euphoric' feeling, where she could now embrace life in the knowledge that James's spirit was watching over her. She continued her painting and looked to the future knowing that the James she knew was him at his happiest. She is now a successful mixed-media artist based in London and has had exhibitions in London and New York. She also now works as an art educator and lecturer. Her pain and sadness from nearly two decades ago has hopefully faded away and the memories she has are cherished.

The friends that surrounded James (unfortunately the book doesn't have the space for the many, many people who played a part in his life) mourned him. Some notable figures were 'Bubbles' Horsley who regarded James as his 'best friend' and missed him terribly. He effectively retired as he certainly had enough money to live the life he chose, and that life is now spent in France with his family. Like Mike Dennett, Horsley still misses James today.

Lord Hesketh has had a remarkable life, starting an airline which he sold for profit after his years in motor-sport. He also sold Easton Neston and all momentoes of Hesketh Racing to a Russian investor for around £16 million, and as a member of the House of Lords, he became quite unfluential in Magaret Thatcher's Conservative government in the late 80s and early 90s, holding the office of Parliamentary Under-Secretary of State at the Department of the Environment, Minister of State at the Department of Trade and Industry and Government Chief Whip at the House of Lords.

John Hogan, who at times was instrumental in helping James climb the motor-sporting ladder, became a senior figure at Philip Morris International and arranged the numerous sponsorship deals that Marlboro had in place in Formula One before tobacco advertising was banned.

Murray Walker has fond memories of James Hunt, but those memories are touched with a hint of realism as he remembers all too well the faults that accompanied the legends. Walker continued to commentate for the BBC (Jonathan Palmer replacing James Hunt at first in the co-role) and then for ITV when they won the rights. He retired from broadcasting a few years ago, but still retains the almost boyish enthusiasm for the sport and attends races when he can or sometimes prefers to sit in his impressive home in Hampshire and enjoy the television coverage. Walker has become a true legend in broadcasting terms and every commentator who now takes on his role is inevitably compared to him.

As for the teams that James raced for in Formula One? Well Hesketh continued for a couple more years after he left, although it was very much a scaled-down version, especially without the input of Lord Hesketh. 'Bubbles' Horsley kept the flag flying with drivers such as Rupert Keegan, Guy Edwards, Harold Ertl, Eddie Cheever and Derek Daly, but sadly the glory of their victory in Holland in 1975 was never close to being repeated. The team finally closed its doors at the end of 1978 after struggling at the back of the pack throughout. They even embraced sponsorship, something which Hesketh himself refused to do as he preferred his cars to be virgin white with blue and red patriotic trimmings, but the sight of a Penthouse logo with a scantily-clad lady across the nose-cone was slightly tacky, even by Formula One standards.

The McLaren team that took Hunt to the 1976 World Championship effectively disappeared at the end of the decade, to be replaced by a slicker and far more professional outfit. Teddy Mayer sold out to Ron Dennis and the Project Four concern and it's fair to say that Dennis introduced a standard in Formula One management never seen before. The McLaren team simply set the standards of professionalism and winning-mentality that had not been visible previously. That new ideal brought about many Championships for Niki Lauda of course, Alain Prost, Ayrton Senna, Mika Hakkinen and Lewis Hamilton. The team that Lauda drove for in the mid-eighties bore no resemblance whatsoever to the one that Hunt drove for a decade earlier. Teddy Mayer went to Indycar racing in the States and was extremely successful right up until his death recently.

Wolf Racing actually never recovered from winning the first Grand Prix they had entered in 1977. By the time James Hunt joined them in 1979, the team was on the slide and after his retirement, they took on future World

Champion Keijo 'Keke' Rosberg. He couldn't improve matters and at the end of the season they sold up to the Copersucar-Fittipaldi outfit, enabling that team to run two cars with a team-mate for Emerson. It didn't last and Fittipaldi continued to struggle until they too closed their doors for the last time.

For Niki Lauda, well of course his story goes on and indeed the famous name of Lauda is still seen on the racetrack, but now with Matthias. Managed by Lukas, he followed his father's footsteps by refusing to listen when Niki told him he would not allow any of his sons to go racing. This stance was of course backed by their mother, Marlene, but Matthias had the steely determination handed down and went ahead anyway. He made his race debut in 2002 in Formula Nissan 2000 and has now had experience of single-seater racing in Formula VW, Formula Three and 2000 and also represented Austria in the ill-fated A1 Grand Prix series. After failing to make much headway in terms of hard results, he moved to touring cars. It is unlikely he will have anything like the success of his father, but Matthias and Luke make a formidable partnership and are surely prepared to write their own story in the Lauda saga.

Of the people who helped Lauda in his career, Willy Dungl was almost an unheralded hero. Credited with helping him recover from the fearsome injuries sustained in 1976 at the German Grand Prix, he stayed alongside the Austrian and helped him attain the level of fitness required when he returned in the early 80s. Dungl was also instrumental in helping the fitness levels of Gerhard Berger, Johnny Herbert, Karl Wendlinger, Martin Donnelly and a certain Michael Schumacher. His dietary ideas helped a generation of racing drivers reach a standard in physical and emotional fitness not seen before, and for that reason was also found to be helping and working with the Austrian skiing team, plus various tennis players. Sadly a kidney problem resulted in a transplant in 1985 and in 2002 he died at the age of 64. His Dungl Clinic, based in Gars am Kamp, is renowned and treats sportsmen and women from all over the world.

The teams that saw Lauda in their Formula One cockpit have had varying fortunes. March continued in a haphazard fashion in Formula One for many years and recording some notable results, without really troubling either of the World Championships. They continued in the top tier of motor racing in various guises until 1992 when a March car, driven at different times by

Karl Wendlinger, Emanuele Naspetti and Jan Lammers, finished ninth in the standings. March has had enormous success in the United States and is still regarded as an iconic name in the sport. Of the founders, a certain Max Mosley rose to the dizzy heights of FIA President and was a major influence in transforming the safety standards of the sport. A controversial figure at times, he ruled F1 with a disarming smile, an educated tongue and an iron fist. The sport has a lot to be grateful to him for.

BRM faded away and are now just a pleasant reminder of the days of 'gentleman' racing. Even when Niki was racing for them, they were living on past glories. The image of a racing green car representing Britain at circuits around the world belongs to the heyday of the 50s and sadly had no place in the cut-throat world of modern Formula One.

Of course one team who have transcended every era are Ferrari. The only team to have competed in every season of F1, they are of course the main 'powerhouse' of the sport, and have had more than a minor say in the way it has been run and the rules that are implemented. It is fair to say that if 'the Prancing Horse' was ever to walk away from Formula One, then the sport would survive, but would be the poorer for it.

After Lauda's departure, the team had another of those droughts that are self-inflicted from time to time. They won the driver's title in 79 with Jody Scheckter, but then produced a selection of some of the most uncompetitive and frankly disastrous Formula One cars in their history. They struggled on with the talents of Gilles Villeneuve, Alain Prost and Nigel Mansell, but came nowhere near the success they demanded until the arrival of the Todt/Brawn/Schumacher partnership in the 1990s. Five World titles followed and then another for the Finn Kimi Raikkonen showed that they are still a force to be reckoned with. They may always be at the behest of a typical Latin temperament in the way the team is run, but it is part of the allure and it has at times served them well. Ferrari is by far and away the most popular team in the sport in terms of fan base and news copy. It will surely continue that way for many years to come.

McLaren have already been described, but the Brabham team that Lauda drove for didn't last long. They took Nelson Piquet to two World titles and arguably created one of the fastest and most powerful cars ever to race in

Formula One the BT52 (and they re-introduced the idea of pit stops into the sport), all under the leadership of the brilliant Gordon Murray, but by the late 80s they had become a shadow of their former selves. Owner Bernie Ecclestone had bigger ideas than just owning a Formula One team and in 1988 he sold the team, who went on under the Middlebridge name and then just faded away. Ecclestone of course became the most powerful man the sport has seen, and transformed it from the haphazard, periphal activity that generated interest, excitement but little revenue into the globally-marketed professional brand that it is today. Many people have become rich due to his business-brilliance and the sport is alive entirely due to his vision, but he is a man that few know and maybe fewer really understand.

Of course the sport of Formula One has changed beyond recognition from the one that so attracted James Hunt and Niki Lauda in the early 1970s. Always regarded as the pinnacle of motor-sport, it was an era when drivers would drive anything anywhere, often appearing at lesser events to supplement their income, and Grand Prix weekends could see a rag-bag number of drivers who would appear annually at their home race, providing they had the resources to polish an old F1 car and qualify it, albeit at the back of the grid. The big teams were there of course, Ferrari, Lotus, McLaren, Tyrrell et al, but their operations were minute compared to today's standards. There were no huge transporters or hospitality motor-homes emblazoned with sponsors names, brilliantly shined to perfection so as not to besmirch the image of the Ecclestone-driven F1 brand. Instead the cars were either pulled on a trailer behind a van, or loaded into a converted bus. The motor-homes were caravans for the drivers to get some peace and quiet before a race and the hundreds of staff that follow a team in the present day were absent back in the 70s. A handful of mechanics (in some cases just one) and occasionally a driver's wife or girlfriend would supply all that was needed for a team to survive the three days of practice and raceday. Practice (used before qualifying became the accepted term for the session) could go on for hours over two days, and the race was not limited to any specific time, and so a Grand Prix could conceivably last twice as long as today.

The cars, although less cluttered than the present, were powerful but lethal machines. An aluminium cockpit surrounded by petrol tanks that carried around 40 gallons of fuel were frankly rockets on wheels, and were at times fatal hence the number of deaths in the sport. The circuits too left a lot to be desired and on many occasions the organisers just simply refused to implement any extra safety measures, knowing that if a driver didn't start the race, he wouldn't receive his starting fee. Jackie Stewart's safety revolution took a long time in coming, but it made the whole difference. Even in the mid-seventies era of Hunt and Lauda when they raced each other, there were no run-off areas should a car spin, but instead someone had the brilliant idea of catch-fencing held up by wooden poles. In a way though it was an improvement on the straw bales so beloved of the 'golden era' of the 50s. At one stage the Americans came up with the excellent idea of discarded tyres to cushion any impact a car may have should it leave the circuit at speed. They were called rather quaintly 'spherical elasticated attenuators'.

Sponsorship existed, but it was almost exclusively from tobacco manufacturers with the occasional petrol company, and aerodynamics were still very much in their infancy, although by the time the Lotus 79 appeared in 1978, it was clear that the sport had mastered the idea.

Some would say the racing was better and the results were less predictable than today, and in fact the 1976 season does bear scrutiny, even though Hunt and Lauda won most of the Grands Prix between them, but it is worth noting that one of the most famous Grands Prix of all time – the 1971 Italian where the first five drivers, led by Peter Gethin, finished within a second of each other – only saw six cars finish, and in one Grand Prix the 1968 German Jackie Stewart won by nearly four minutes!

In the mid-seventies, television coverage was minimal, and in the UK, only the British Grand Prix was shown live. It wasn't until 1978 that a regular highlights programme was shown on the BBC, usually around thirty minutes and shown on the evening of the race. It is no co-incidence that this was shortly after the tremendous 1976 season, and it is fair to say that the battle between Hunt and Lauda that year opened the eyes of the sporting world to Formula One. It had predominantly been the exclusive interest of European enthusiasts, in fact nearly every race was held in Europe with a few 'long haul' ones in North and South America and Japan, but as time went by, and the sport transformed itself into the global brand and professionalism we see today, it naturally expanded to areas that had previously no interest whatsoever in motor racing.

As alluded to many times, one of the biggest changes in Formula One has been the increase in safety measures. 1976 was the first season there had not been a fatality in the sport although Lauda's accident nearly continued that sorry statistic but sadly the deaths continued unabated seemingly until the mid-eighties. In fact Ayrton Senna's tragic accident at Imola in 1994 was thankfully the last fatality in F1 at the time of writing. Hopefully that is a statistic that continues.

Formula One is still the sport it was, except now it is played out to a bigger audience and at a higher level. The stakes are the same, but the punishment is now not as harsh.

CHAPTER THIRTY FIVE

The Final Chapter

James Hunt and Niki Lauda were disparate personalities, but they left their indelible mark on the sport they graced. Neither could be described as 'greats', but what they achieved was certainly great.

For Hunt, his behaviour off the track was the making of him and the downfall of him. The fact that he was upper-class and spoke well, was probably one of the reasons why he was indulged when his excesses crossed the natural border that most adhere to. It is fair to say that if he was of a lower-class upbringing, he would be regarded in very much the way that teenagers are when seen on many a night out in any city or town centre. They and he would be derided and not tolerated. It also helped that he could be charming when questioned, and his way with women gave him the nerve to do things that many only think of. He was the archetype playboy racing-driver, the kind that everyone thinks should be as opposed to the ones of modern day who live a corporate and seemingly soulless existence. In recent years only one driver, Kimi Raikkonen, has managed to attract the kind of headlines that Hunt embraced, and Raikkonen is Hunt's biggest fan! He actually entered rallying events when he was younger under the name of 'James Hunt' and also has a helmet with his name emblazoned, which occasionally he wears at a Grand Prix, but he is just a small hill compared to the mountain that made James Hunt the man he was. For modern Formula One fans, it is difficult to explain how popular he was in the 70s and how every move he made became both back and front page headlines. He was the David Beckham of the era, except he didn't embrace the family-loving, clean-cut image that Beckham has nurtured. For Hunt, life was for living, and he had a great time doing it.

On the track he was talented, but no more. He had the ability to drive a racing car fast, and on his day he could beat anyone, but his day only came occasionally. His 1976 World Championship owed as much to sheer force of personality and will-power as it did to pure talent. His car was no better or worse than the Ferrari through the season, and it has to be remembered that he finished the same number of races as Lauda leading up to the final Grand Prix in Japan, but won more. Some would say that his title was tainted due to Lauda missing two races due to his injuries, but let's not forget the penalties imposed on Hunt, including losing the British Grand Prix victory, and it may sound harsh, but it was Niki Lauda who crashed at the Nurburgring, not James Hunt. In fact Hunt went on to win the restarted race.

The author makes no apologies for admitting that James Hunt was his own personal sporting hero (plus a footballer who played for his favourite team), but I approached Formula One properly just as Hunt's star was fading fast. I'd seen him win the 1977 British Grand Prix at Silverstone, but one year later witnessed one of the too-many low points in his career. In an age before the internet or twenty-four hour rolling news on radio or television, I stood at Brands Hatch and listened to the PA man giving out the grid a few hours before the race, and waited and waited until his name was mentioned. He'd qualified 14th, unbelievably bad for a car that wasn't that uncompetitive. No worries, I reasoned, he will make a charge through the grid and win anyway (I'd actually seen him walking behind the main stand that morning without any shoes on and completely ignored by most spectators. Would it be possible for that to happen today?). He crashed on the eighth lap for no reason whatsoever and afterwards there were rumours and accusations that he was still suffering the effects of a drug-fuelled evening. That was strenuously denied, but it was a heartbreaking way to say goodbye to a true British sporting hero. He didn't race in a British Grand Prix again.

When he retired, there was a feeling that he had made the right choice. The events of the 1978 Italian Grand Prix had disturbed him greatly, and for those who followed his exploits on the track (and tried to ignore the stories off the track), it was clear he wasn't the racer he was. The Wolf car was a shambles and seeing a former World Champion struggling is never easy on the eye. It gave reminders of the great Graham Hill who most believed raced on for far too long and became sadly uncompetitive against drivers who in the past should not have been on the same circuit as him. It felt the same with James.

His broadcasting career was a triumph. I sometimes find myself amazed that he worked in the same building as myself and I just wish I'd managed to meet him at that time, but our paths never crossed. I have got to know Murray

Walker, and his stories and memories are wonderful to hear. Murray genuinely liked James toward the end of his life and it was heartbreaking for him when he died.

It was also heartbreaking to have to listen to all of the sordid stories concerning his life when he died. The media (of which admittedly I belong) decided to resurrect the 'Shunt' title whenever they spoke of him and his World Championship just seemed to be a passing diversion. He was never a 'great', but in my eyes he was the greatest. It's an old cliché, but simply there will never be another quite like him, no matter how hard the likes of the extremely-likeable Kimi Raikkonen try. God rest James, you gave us all a lot of pleasure.

In a way Niki Lauda was the antithesis of James Hunt both on and off the track. Off it, he didn't court the lifestyle and ultimately the controversy that his great friend did. The only time he seemed to spend as much time on the front pages as the back was in 1976 when he married Marlene, but that was inevitably overshadowed by the James/Suzy/Richard Burton saga, and in fact only the Austrian press seemed to be interested. He of course made all the headlines shortly afterwards with his horrific crash in Germany.

That was of course a defining moment for the man. The injuries suffered and the incredible recovery is the like normally seen on the battlefield, and not in a sporting arena, albeit one as dangerous as mid-seventies motor racing. It is hard to believe that any of today's racers would show the same type of fortitude as Lauda, and it is particularly saddening to remember how little understanding there was from the hierarchy at Ferrari at that time. His comeback is literally the story of a legend and the fact that he went on to win two more titles (and many believe he would have won in 1976 had he not crashed at the Nurburgring) is simply awe-inspiring.

Whereas James Hunt was impulsive and unpredictable on and off the circuit, Lauda was anything but. In his early days he did go against convention and his increasing mount of debt pays testament to that, but his incredible inner-belief meant that he always knew he would make a success of his chosen profession. Once he'd got himself into the position of being comfortable with his lifestyle and he started chasing Championship-glory, his analytical mind took over and he drove to win, even if that meant driving as conservatively as possible. His critics would say that he was never the most exciting of drivers and compare him to his early team-mate at McLaren, Alain Prost, but that is a comparison worth having. A record of three World Championships and 25 Grand Prix victories from just 171 starts is impressive whichever way you look at it. It also compares quite favourably with Hunt's one World Championship and 10 victories from 92 starts.

Of course Lauda is now equally as well known as an aviator and his battles with the huge Austrian Airlines (of which he finally lost after many years) again showed the incredible resilience of the man. To then pick himself up and start all over again with a new airline company shows that he is never beaten, but of course there have been failings. The brief period at Jaguar didn't exactly show him in the best of lights and the shambles the team became seemed to owe as much to his management as it did to the Ford hierarchy who appeared to be completely unaware of what constitutes a successful Formula One team.

Both drivers have reached legendary status, and maybe both for entirely different reasons. I loved James Hunt and at the time probably disliked Niki Lauda, mainly because he was seen as a main rival to our British sporting hero, but as the years have progressed, I have appreciated what a tremendous sportsman and human being he was and still is. James left us some time ago, but left a great legacy and many, many memories, whereas Niki survived the worst possible accident and is still there at the Grand Prix paddock talking in his clipped Austrian accent and telling it the way it is like he always has. In my eyes, both are true legends.

STATISTICS

Formula One

1971
Austrian Grand Prix 15th August
Lauda (March711) qualified 21st, retired engine

1972
Argentinian Grand Prix 23rd January
Lauda (March721) qualified 22nd, finished 11th
South African Grand Prix 4th March
Lauda (March721) qualified 21st, finished 7th
Spanish Grand Prix 1st May
Lauda (March721) qualified 25th, retired, jammed throttle
Monaco Grand Prix 14th May
Lauda (March721) qualified 22nd, finished 16th
Belgian Grand Prix 4th June
Lauda (March721) qualified 25th, finished 12th
French Grand Prix 2nd July
Lauda (March721) qualified 21st, retired, rear suspension
British Grand Prix 15th July
Lauda (March721) qualified 19th, finished 9th
German Grand Prix 30th July
Lauda (March721) qualified 23rd, retired, oil leak
Austrian Grand Prix 13th August
Lauda (March721) qualified 21st, finished 10th
Italian Grand Prix 10th September
Lauda (March721) qualified 20th, finished 13th
Canadian Grand Prix 24th September
Lauda (March721) qualified 19th, disqualified
US Grand Prix (East) 8th October
Lauda (March721) qualified 25th, finished 17th

1973
Argentinian Grand Prix 28th January
Lauda (BRM160) qualified 13th, retired, engine failure
Brazilian Grand Prix 11th February
Lauda (BRM160) qualified 13th, finished 8th
South African Grand Prix 3rd March
Lauda (BRM160) qualified 10th, retired, engine failure
Spanish Grand Prix 29th April
Lauda (BRM160) qualified 10th, retired, wheel problems
Belgian Grand Prix 20th May
Lauda (BRM160) qualified 14th, finished 5th
Monaco Grand Prix 3rd June
Lauda (BRM160) qualified 6th, retired, gearbox
Hunt (March731) qualified 18th, retired, engine failure
Swedish Grand Prix 17th June
Lauda (BRM160) qualified 15th, finished 13th
French Grand Prix 1st July
Lauda (BRM160) qualified 17th, finished 9th
Hunt (March731) qualified 14th, finished 6th
British Grand Prix 14th July
Lauda (BRM160) qualified 9th, finished 12th
Hunt (March731) qualified 11th, finished 4th
Dutch Grand Prix 29th July
Lauda (BRM160) - qualified 11th, retired, fuel pump
Hunt (March731) qualified 7th, finished 3rd
German Grand Prix 5th August
Lauda (BRM160) qualified 5th, accident
Austrian Grand Prix 19th August
Lauda (BRM160) withdrew through injury
Hunt (March731) qualified 9th, retired, fuel problems
Italian Grand Prix 9th September
Lauda (BRM160) qualified 15th, accident
Hunt (March731) withdrew after accident
Canadian Grand Prix 23rd September
Lauda (BRM160) qualified 8th, retired, engine problems
Hunt (March731) qualified 15th, finished 7th

US Grand Prix (East) 7th October
Lauda (BRM160) qualified 21st, retired, oil pressure
Hunt (March731) qualified 4th, finished 2nd

1974
Argentinian Grand Prix 13th January
Lauda (Ferrari312) qualified 8th, finished 2nd
Hunt (March731) qualified 5th, retired, engine overheating
Brazilian Grand Prix 27th January
Lauda (Ferrari312) qualified 3rd, retired, engine failure
South African Grand Prix 30th March
Lauda (Ferrari312) pole position, retired ignition
Hunt (Hesketh308) qualified 14th, retired cv joint
Spanish Grand Prix 28th April
Lauda (Ferrari312) pole position, **winner**
Hunt (Hesketh308) qualified 10th, finished 10th
Belgian Grand Prix 12th May
Lauda (Ferrari312) qualified 3rd, finished 2nd
Hunt (Hesketh308) qualified 9th, retired, suspension failure
Monaco Grand Prix 26th May
Lauda (Ferrari312) pole position, retired, alternator
Hunt (Hesketh308) qualified 7th, retired, driveshaft
Swedish Grand Prix 9th June
Lauda (Ferrari312) qualified 3rd, retired, gearbox
Hunt (Hesketh308) qualified 6th, finished 3rd
Dutch Grand Prix 23rd June
Lauda (Ferrari312) pole position, **winner**
Hunt (Hesketh308) qualified 6th, accident
French Grand Prix 7th July
Lauda (Ferrari312) pole position, finished 2nd
Hunt (Hesketh308) qualified 10th, accident
British Grand Prix 20th July
Lauda (Ferrari312) pole position, finished 5th
Hunt (Hesketh) qualified 6th, retired, suspension failure
German Grand Prix 4th August
Lauda (Ferrari312) pole position, accident
Hunt (Hesketh308) qualified 13th, retired, gearbox failure

Austrian Grand Prix 18th August
Lauda (Ferrari312) pole position, retired, engine failure
Hunt (Hesketh308) qualified 7th, finished 3rd
Italian Grand Prix 8th September
Lauda (Ferrari312) pole position, retired, engine failure
Hunt (Hesketh308) qualified 8th, retired, engine failure
Canadian Grand Prix 22nd September
Lauda (Ferrari312) qualified 2nd, accident
Hunt (Hesketh308) qualified 8th, finished 4th
US Grand Prix (East) 6th October
Lauda (Ferrari312) qualified 5th, retired, tyres
Hunt (Hesketh308) qualified 2nd, finished 3rd

1975
Argentinian Grand Prix 12th January
Lauda (Ferrari312) qualified 4th, finished 6th
Hunt (Hesketh308) qualified 6th, finished 2nd
Brazilian Grand Prix 26th January
Lauda (Ferrari312) qualified 4th, finished 5th
Hunt (Hesketh308) qualified 7th, finished 6th
South African Grand Prix 1st March
Lauda (Ferrari312) qualified 4th, finished 5th
Hunt (Hesketh308) qualified 12th, retired, fuel problems
Spanish Grand Prix 27th April
Lauda (Ferrari312) pole position, accident
Hunt (Hesketh308) qualified 3rd, accident
Monaco Grand Prix 11th May
Lauda (Ferrari312) pole position, **winner**
Hunt (Hesketh308) qualified 11th, accident
Belgian Grand Prix 25th May
Lauda (Ferrari312) pole position, **winner**
Hunt (Hesketh308) qualified 11th, retired, gear linkage
Swedish Grand Prix 8th June
Lauda (Ferrari312) qualified 6th, **winner**
Hunt (Hesketh308) qualified 13th, retired, brakes
Dutch Grand Prix 22nd June
Lauda (Ferrari312) pole position, finished 2nd
Hunt (Hesketh308) qualified 3rd, **winner**

French Grand Prix 6th July
Lauda (Ferrari312) pole position, **winner**
Hunt (Hesketh308) qualified 3rd, finished 2nd
British Grand Prix 19th July
Lauda (Ferrari312) qualified 3rd, finished 8th
Hunt (Hesketh308) qualified 9th, finished 4th
German Grand Prix 3rd August
Lauda (Ferrari312) pole position, finished 3rd
Hunt (Hesketh308) qualified 9th, retired, wheel problems
Austrian Grand Prix 17th August
Lauda (Ferrari312) pole position, finished 6th
Hunt (Hesketh308) qualified 2nd, finished 2nd
Italian Grand Prix 7th September
Lauda (Ferrari312) pole position, finished 3rd
Hunt (Hesketh308) qualified 8th, finshed 5th
US Grand Prix (East) 5th October
Lauda (Ferrari312) pole position **winner**
Hunt (Hesketh308) qualified 15th, finished 4th

1976
Brazilian Grand Prix 25th January
Lauda (Ferrari312) qualified 2nd, **winner**
Hunt (McLarenM23) pole position, retired, throttle
South African Grand Prix 6th March
Lauda (Ferrari312) qualified 2nd, **winner**
Hunt (McLarenM23) pole position, finished 2nd
US Grand Prix (West) 28th March
Lauda (Ferrari312) qualified 4th, finished 2nd
Hunt (McLarenM23) qualified 3rd, accident
Spanish Grand Prix 2nd May
Lauda (Ferrari312) qualified 2nd, finished 2nd
Hunt (McLarenM23) pole position, **winner**
Belgian Grand Prix 16th May
Lauda (Ferrari312) pole position, **winner**
Hunt (McLarenM23) qualified 3rd, retired, gearbox

Monaco Grand Prix 30th May
Lauda (Ferrari312) pole position, **winner**
Hunt (McLarenM23) qualified 14th, finished 8th

Swedish Grand Prix 13th June
Lauda (Ferrari312) qualified 5th, finished 3rd
Hunt (McLarenM23) qualified 8th, finished 5th

French Grand Prix 4th July
Lauda (Ferrari312) qualified 2nd, retired, engine failure
Hunt (McLarenM23) pole position, **winner**

British Grand Prix 18th July
Lauda (Ferrari312) pole position, **winner**
Hunt (McLarenM23) qualified 2nd, disqualified

German Grand Prix 1st August
Lauda (Ferrari312) qualified 2nd, accident
Hunt (McLarenM23) pole position, **winner**

Austrian Grand Prix 15th August
Hunt (McLarenM23) pole position, finished 4th

Dutch Grand Prix 29th August
Hunt (McLarenM23) qualified 2nd, **winner**

Italian Grand Prix 12th September
Lauda (Ferrari312) qualified 5th, finished 4th
Hunt (McLarenM23) qualified 25th, accident

Canadian Grand Prix 3rd October
Lauda (Ferrari312) qualified 6th, finished 8th
Hunt (McLarenM23) pole position, **winner**

US Grand Prix (East) 10th October
Lauda (Ferrari312) qualified 5th, finished 3rd
Hunt (McLarenM23) pole position, **winner**

Japanese Grand Prix 24th October
Lauda (Ferrari312) qualified 3rd, withdrew
Hunt (McLarenM23) qualified 2nd, finished 3rd

1977

Argentinian Grand Prix 9th January
Lauda (Ferrari312) qualified 4th, retired, oil pressure
Hunt (McLarenM23) pole position, retired, suspension

Brazilian Grand Prix 23rd January
Lauda (Ferrari312) qualified 15th, finished 3rd
Hunt (McLarenM23) pole position, finished 2nd

South African Grand Prix 5th March
Lauda (Ferrari312) qualified 3rd, **winner**
Hunt (McLarenM23) pole position, finished 4th

US Grand Prix (West) 3rd April
Lauda (Ferrari312) pole position, finished 2nd
Hunt (McLarenM23) qualified 8th, finished 7th

Spanish Grand Prix 8th May
Lauda (Ferrari312) qualified 3rd, injured
Hunt (McLarenM26) qualified 7th, retired, engine

Monaco Grand Prix 22nd May
Lauda (Ferrari312) qualified 6th, finished 2nd
Hunt (McLarenM26) qualified 7th, retired, engine

Belgian Grand Prix 5th June
Lauda (Ferrari312) qualified 13th, finished 2nd
Hunt (McLarenM23 and M26) qualified 9th, finished 7th

Swedish Grand Prix 19th June
Lauda (Ferrari312) qualified 15th, retired, tyres
Hunt (McLarenM26) qualified 3rd, finished 12th

French Grand Prix 3rd July
Lauda (Ferrari312) qualified 11th, finished 5th
Hunt (McLarenM26) qualified 2nd, finished 3rd

British Grand Prix 16th July
Lauda (Ferrari312) qualified 3rd, finished 2nd
Hunt (McLarenM26) pole position, **winner**

German Grand Prix 31st July
Lauda (Ferrari312) qualified 3rd, **winner**
Hunt (McLarenM26) qualified 4th, retired, fuel pump

Austrian Grand Prix –14th August
Lauda (Ferrari312) pole position, finished 2nd
Hunt (McLarenM26) qualified 2nd, retired, engine failure

Dutch Grand Prix 28th August
Lauda (Ferrari312) qualified 4th, **winner**
Hunt (McLarenM26) qualified 3rd, accident

Italian Grand Prix 11th September
Lauda (Ferrari312) qualified 5th, finished 2nd
Hunt (McLarenM26) pole position, accident
US Grand Prix (East) 2nd October
Lauda (Ferrari312) qualified 9th, finished 4th
Hunt (McLarenM26) pole position, **winner**
Canadian Grand Prix 9th October
Hunt (McLarenM26) qualified 2nd, accident
Japanese Grand Prix 23rd October
Hunt (McLarenM26) qualified 2nd, **winner**

1978
Argentinian Grand Prix 15th January
Lauda (BrabhamBT45) qualified 5th, finished 2nd
Hunt (McLarenM26) qualified 6th, finished 4th
Brazilian Grand Prix 29th January
Lauda (BrabhamBT45) qualified 10th, finished 3rd
Hunt (McLarenM26) qualified 2nd, accident
South African Grand Prix 4th March
Lauda (BrabhamBT46) pole position, retired, engine falure
Hunt (McLarenM26) qualified 3rd, retired, engine failure
US Grand Prix (West) 2nd April
Lauda (BrabhmaBT 46) qualified 3rd, retired, ignition
Hunt (McLarenM26) qualified 7th, accident
Monaco Grand Prix 7th May
Lauda (BrabhamBT46) qualified 3rd, finished 2nd
Hunt (McLarenM26) qualified 6th, retired, handling
Belgian Grand Prix 21st May
Lauda (BrabhamBT46) qualified 3rd, accident
Hunt (McLarenM26) qualified 6th, accident
Spanish Grand Prix 4th June
Lauda (BrabhamBT46) qualified 6th, retired, engine failure
Hunt (McLarenM26) qualified 4th, finished 6th
Swedish Grand Prix 17th June
Lauda (BrabhamBT46) qualified 3rd, **winner**
Hunt (McLarenM26) qualified 14th, finished 8th

French Grand Prix 2nd July
Lauda (BrabhamBT46) qualified 3rd, retired, engine failure
Hunt (McLarenM26) qualified 4th, finished 3rd
British Grand Prix 16th July
Lauda (BrabhamBT46) qualified 4th, finished 2nd
Hunt (McLarenM26) qualified 14th, accident
German Grand Prix 30th July
Lauda (BrabhamBT46) qualified 3rd, retired, engine failure
Hunt (McLarenM26) qualified 8th, disqualified
Austrian Grand Prix 13th August
Lauda (BrabhamBT46) – qualified 12th, accident
Hunt (McLarenM26) qualified 8th, accident
Dutch Grand Prix 27th August
Lauda (BrabhamBT46) qualified 3rd, finished 3rd
Hunt (McLarenM26) qualified 7th, finished 10th
Italian Grand Prix 10th September
Lauda (BrabhamBT46) qualified 4th, **winner**
Hunt (McLarenM26) qualified 10th, retired, distributor
US Grand Prix (East) 1st October
Lauda (BrabhamBT46) qualified 5th, retired, engine failure
Hunt (McLarenM26) qualified 6th, finished 7th
Canadian Grand Prix 8th October
Lauda (BrabhamBT46) qualified 7th, retired, brakes
Hunt (McLarenM26) qualified 19th, accident

1979
Argentinian Grand Prix 21st January
Lauda (BrabhamBT48) qualified 22nd, retired, fuel pressure
Hunt (WolfWR7) qualified 18th, retired, electrics
Brazilian Grand Prix 4th February
Lauda (BrabhamBT48) qualified 12th, retired, gearbox
Hunt (WolfWR7) qualified 10th, retired, steering
South African Grand Prix 3rd March
Lauda (BrabhamBT48) qualified 4th, finished 6th
Hunt (WolfWR7) qualified 13th, finished 8th

US Grand Prix (West) - 8th April
Lauda (BrabhamBT48) qualified 11th, accident
Hunt (WolfWR7) qualified 8th, retired, driveshaft
Spanish Grand Prix 29th April
Lauda (BrabhamBT48) qualified 6th, retired, oil leak
Hunt (WolfWR7 and WR8) qualified 15th, retired, brakes
Belgian Grand Prix 13th May
Lauda (BrabhamBT48) qualified 13th, retired, engine failure
Hunt (Wolf WR8) qualified 9th, accident
Monaco Grand Prix 27th May
Lauda (BrabhamBT48) qualified 4th, accident
Hunt (WolfWR7) qualified 10th, retired, cv joint
French Grand Prix 1st July
Lauda (BrabhamBT48) qualified 6th, accident
British Grand Prix 14th July
Lauda (BrabhamBT48) qualified 6th, retired, brakes
German Grand Prix 29th July
Lauda (BrabhamBT48) qualified 7th, retired, brakes
Austrian Grand Prix 12th August
Lauda (BrabhamBT48) qualified 4th, retired, oil leak
Dutch Grand Prix 26th August
Lauda (BrabhamBT48) qualified 9th, injured
Italian Grand Prix 9th September
Lauda (BrabhamBT48) qualified 7th, finished 4th

1982
South African Grand Prix 23rd January
Lauda (McLarenMP4) qualified 13th, finished 4th
Brazilian Grand Prix 21st March
Lauda (McLarenMP4) qualified 5th, accident
US Grand Prix (West) 4th April
Lauda (McLarenMP4) qualified 2nd, **winner**
San Marino Grand Prix 25th April
Lauda (McLarenMP4) - withdrew
Belgian Grand Prix 9th May
Lauda (McLarenMP4) qualified 4th, disqualified

Monaco Grand Prix 23rd May
Lauda (McLarenMP4) qualified 12th, retired, engine failure
US Grand Prix (East) 6th June
Lauda (McLarenMP4) qualified 10th, accident
Canadian Grand Prix 13th June
Lauda (McLarenMP4) qualified 11th, retired, clutch
Dutch Grand Prix 3rd July
Lauda (McLarenMP4) qualified 5th, finished 4th
British Grand Prix 18th July
Lauda (McLarenMP4) qualified 5th, **winner**
French Grand Prix 25th July
Lauda (McLarenMP4) qualified 9th, finished 8th
German Grand Prix 8th August
Lauda (McLarenMP4) injured
Austrian Grand Prix 15th August
Lauda (McLarenMP4) qualified 10th, finished 5th
Swiss Grand Prix 29th August
Lauda (McLarenMP4) qualified 4th, finished 3rd
Italian Grand Prix 10th September
Lauda (McLarenMP4) qualified 10th, retired, tyres
Las Vegas Grand Prix 25th September
Lauda (McLarenMP4) qualified 13th, retired, engine failure

1983
Brazilian Grand Prix 13th March
Lauda (McLarenMP4) qualified 9th, finished 3rd
US Grand Prix (West) 27th March
Lauda (McLarenMP4) qualified 23rd, finished 2nd
French Grand Prix 17th April
Lauda (McLarenMP4) qualified 11th, retired, wheel bearing
San Marino Grand Prix 1st May
Lauda (McLarenMP4) qualified 17th, accident
Monaco Grand Prix 15th May
Lauda (McLarenMP4) did not qualify
Belgian Grand Prix 22nd May
Lauda (McLarenMP4) qualified 15th, retired, engine failure

US Grand Prix (East) 5th June
Lauda (McLarenMP4) qualified 18th, retired, suspension
Canadian Grand Prix 12th June
Lauda (McLarenMP4) qualified 19th, accident
British Grand Prix 16th July
Lauda (McLarenMP4) qualified 15th, finished 6th
German Grand Prix 7th August
Lauda (McLarenMP4) qualified 18th, disqualified
Austrian Grand Prix 14th August
Lauda (McLarenMP4) qualified 14th, finished 6th
Dutch Grand Prix 28th August
Lauda (McLarenMP4) qualified 19th, retired, brakes
Italian Grand Prix 11th September
Lauda (McLarenMP4) qualified 13th, retired, electrics
European Grand Prix 25th September
Lauda (McLarenMP4) qualified 13th, retired, engine failure
South African Grand Prix 15th October
Lauda (McLarenMP4) qualified 12th, retired, electrics

1984
Brazilian Grand Prix 25th March
Lauda (McLarenMP4) qualified 6th, retired, electrics
South African Grand Prix 7th April
Lauda (McLarenMP4) qualified 8th, **winner**
Belgian Grand Prix 29th April
Lauda (McLarenMP4) qualified 13th, retired, water pump
San Marino Grand Prix 6th May
Lauda (McLarenMP4) qualified 5th, retired, engine failure
French Grand Prix 20th May
Lauda (McLarenMP4) qualified 9th, **winner**
Monaco Grand Prix 3rd June
Lauda (McLarenMP4) qualified 7th, accident
Canadian Grand Prix 17th June
Lauda (McLarenMP4) qualified 7th, finished 2nd
US Grand Prix (East) 24th June
Lauda (McLarenMP4) qualified 9th, retired, electrics

Dallas Grand Prix 8th July
Lauda (McLarenMP4) qualified 5th, accident
British Grand Prix 22nd July
Lauda (McLarenMP4) qualified 3rd, **winner**
German Grand Prix 5th August
Lauda (McLarenMP4) qualified 7th, finished 2nd
Austrian Grand Prix 19th August
Lauda (McLarenMP4) qualified 4th, **winner**
Dutch Grand Prix 26th August
Lauda (McLarenMP4) qualified 6th, finished 2nd
Italian Grand Prix 9th September
Lauda (McLarenMP4) qualified 4th, **winner**
European Grand Prix 7th October
Lauda (McLarenMP4) qualified 15th, finished 4th
Portuguese Grand Prix 21st October
Lauda (McLarenMP4) qualified 11th, finished 2nd

1985
Brazilian Grand Prix 7th April
Lauda (McLarenMP4) qualified 9th, retired, fuel problems
Portuguese Grand Prix 21st April
Lauda (McLarenMP4) qualified 7th, retired, engine failure
San Marino Grand Prix 5th May
Lauda (McLarenMP4) qualified 7th, finished 4th
Monaco Grand Prix 19th May
Lauda (McLarenMP4) qualified 14th, accident
Canadian Grand Prix 16th June
Lauda (McLarenMP4) qualified 17th, retired, engine failure
US Grand Prix (East) 23rd June
Lauda (McLarenMP4) qualified 12th, retired, brakes
French Grand Prix 7th July
Lauda (McLarenMP4) qualified 6th, retired, gearbox
British Grand Prix 21st July
Lauda (McLarenMP4) qualified 10th, retired, electrics
German Grand Prix 4th August
Lauda (McLarenMP4) qualified 12th, finished 5th

Austrian Grand Prix 18th August
Lauda (McLarenMP4) qualified 3rd, retired, engine failure
Dutch Grand Prix 25th August
Lauda (McLarenMP4) qualified 10th, **winner**
Italian Grand Prix 8th September
Lauda (McLarenMP4) qualified 16th, retired, gearbox
South African Grand Prix 19th October
Lauda (McLarenMP4) qualified 8th, retired, engine failure
Australian Grand Prix 3rd November
Lauda (McLarenMP4) qualified 16th, accident

SEASON-BY-SEASON:

1971	Lauda	0 points	not classified in Championship
1972	Lauda	0 points	not classified in Championship
1973	Lauda	2 points	17th in Championship
	Hunt	14 points	8th in Championship
1974	Lauda	38 points	4th in Championship
	Hunt	15 points	8th in Championship
1975	Lauda	64.5 points	**World Champion**
	Hunt	33 points	4th in Championship
1976	Lauda	68 points	2nd in Championship
	Hunt	69 points	**World Champion**
1977	Lauda	72 points	**World Champion**
	Hunt	40 points	5th in Championship
1978	Lauda	44 points	4th in Championship
	Hunt	8 points	13th in Championship
1979	Lauda	4 points	14th in Championship
	Hunt	0 points	not classified in Championship
1982	Lauda	30 points	5th in Championship
1983	Lauda	12 points	10th in Championship
1984	Lauda	72 points	**World Champion**
1985	Lauda	14 points	10th in Championship

NIKI LAUDA:
171   GRANDS PRIX
3   WORLD CHAMPIONSHIPS
25   VICTORIES
24   POLE POSITIONS

JAMES HUNT:
92   GRANDS PRIX
1   WORLD CHAMPIONSHIP
10   VICTORIES
14   POLE POSITIONS

Made in the USA
Coppell, TX
11 January 2020

14338558R10114